St. Joseph in the Lives of Two Blesseds of the Church

Blessed Junipero Serra
and
Blessed Joseph Marello

Rev. Larry Toschi, OSJ

Guardian of the Redeemer Books
544 West Cliff Drive
Santa Cruz, CA 95060

Guardian of the Redeemer Books
544 West Cliff Drive
Santa Cruz, CA 95060
      (408) 471-1700

Cover designed by Flora Jean Ball
and drawn by Jim Goold

Library of Congress Catalog Number:
94-76450

International Standard Book Number
1-883839-05-X

This Printing: March 25, 1997

CONTENTS

INTRODUCTION

Junipero Serra, the great Franciscan missionary, was born in Mallorca, Spain, in 1713 and died in Monterey, California in 1784. Joseph Marello, bishop of Acqui and founder of the Oblates of St. Joseph, was born in Turin, Italy, in 1844 and died in Savona, Italy, in 1895. What did they have in common?

The title of this small book clearly indicates why they are included together here: St. Joseph, the husband of Mary and virginal father of Jesus, is central to each of their lives. Each was given the name "Joseph" the day of his baptism, and each kept St. Joseph as his patron his whole life long. Both of them exemplify an admirable trust in divine providence, aided by St. Joseph's powerful intercession.

Living in the nineteenth century, Joseph Marello looked to St. Joseph not only as a patron and protector, but also as a model to be imitated. The element of imitation is not found so explicitly in Junipero Serra, who lived in an earlier century, but it is clear that he too learned a profound trust in God's providence from his devotion to St. Joseph.

Another significant fact about these two men is that each has been declared "Blessed" by Pope John

Paul II, in public recognition of their sanctity. The beatifications took place within a five year span on dates that almost coincide: September 25, 1988 for Blessed Serra and September 26, 1993 for Blessed Marello.

The first part of this book was prepared for the Fifth International Symposium on St. Joseph, held in Mexico City, the year after Serra's beatification. The second part was presented at the Sixth International Symposium, held in Rome on the eve of Marello's beatification.

Finally, the author considers himself deeply indebted to both of these Blesseds. As a native Californian, he considers Blessed Serra the father of Christianity in his native state. As an Oblate of St. Joseph, he calls Blessed Marello founder and father of the religious congregation to which he belongs.

May the heroic and holy lives of these two Blesseds lead you also to greater trust in the unfailing kindness of God, under the patronage of St. Joseph.

PART I

ST. JOSEPH
AND BLESSED SERRA,
FOUNDER OF
ALTA CALIFORNIA

(and St. Joseph's presence in other parts
of the northern circumference
of New Spain in the eighteenth century)

Originally given at the Fifth International Symposium on Saint Joseph, held in Mexico City September 17-24, 1989. The presentation was originally published in *Estudios Josefinos*, Volume XLV (1991) Valladolid, Spain; and in *Cahiers de Joséphologie*, Volume XXXIX (1991) Montreal, Canada.

Though indigenous populations had lived in California for many centuries, and though European explorations had taken place earlier, California regards the eighteenth century as the real beginning of its modern existence. Even in a country where Catholics are a minority and where there is adamant insistence on separation of church and state in public display, the name and image of Junipero Serra occur repeatedly to recognize him as the founder of our state. The missions he established remain in their restored form as historical monuments of interest to all. Countless vacationers continue to travel the route of "El Camino Real" that links this chain he founded.

My hope is to bring to light in some small way what is little known to most Californians, and what is certainly not without interest to every devotee of St. Joseph throughout the world. Seldom recognized is the fact that Blessed Father Serra's story in Alta California is in every way St. Joseph's story. From the day of Serra's birth until his last Mass before dying, St. Joseph is present. The expedition to Upper California is under St. Joseph's patronage, and if there is a particular date that should be observed in our history, it is March 19, 1770. Through St. Joseph's intervention on this date, Portolá's expedition cancels plans of abandonment and decides to stay. Our first permanent European secular town was "San José" which is presently the third largest city in the state.

Before developing these points, however, it will be helpful to include something of St. Joseph's presence in the northern and western rim of New Spain. Due to the vastness of this area and the scarcity of documentation, this background will be sketchy at best, while Alta California will be treated in more detail.

THE NORTHERN
CIRCUMFERENCE OF NEW SPAIN

By the sixteenth century devotion to St. Joseph is well established in central México with solemn chapels and processions dedicated to his honor,[1]

[1] G. DE MENDIETA, *Historia Eclesiástica Indiana*, 1596, ch. xx "De las procesiones que salen de la capilla de San José en México y de la majestad de esta capilla," México 1945, 87-91. J. C. CARRILLO-OJEDA, "San José en la Nueva España," *Presencia de San José en el Siglo XVII, Estudios Josefinos* Valladolid 1987, 627-653.

and with apostles such as Friar Juan de Béjar continually preaching about him and promoting his acceptance as patron of all New Spain.[2] Exploration and settlement in the northern frontier stretching from Baja California to Texas is naturally slower, but St. Joseph's name is found in the earliest beginnings of each region.

Sonora and Baja California

St. Joseph's presence may best be chronicled by treating these two areas together, since their histories are so inter-twined.

At least by 1633 we find an island named "San José" off the coast of Baja.[3] In Sonora there are a number of places named after St. Joseph. The following years are approximate and the application of St. Joseph's name is difficult to pinpoint, but early Jesuits are credited with: "San José Mátape" in the Névome River area, 1629;[4] "San José de los

---

[2]MENDIETA, ch. liii "De otros ilustres varones de esta provincia del Santo Evangelio," 158-159.

[3]M. LEON-PORTILLA, *Voyages of Francisco de Ortega, California 1632-1636*, Los Angeles 1973, 45. W. WHEELOCK and H. E. GULICK, *Baja California Guidebook*, Glendale California 1980, 210. F. J. ALEGRE, *Historia de la Provincia de la Compañía de Jesús de Nueva España*, Rome 1956, 12. T. ROBERTSON, *Baja California and its Missions*, Glendale 1978, 12.

[4]P. M. ROCA, *Paths of the Padres Through Sonora*, Tucson Arizona 1967, 8,240-242. G. B. ECKHART, *Guide to the History of the Missions of Sonora, 1646-1826*, Tucson 1961, 13.

Pimas" on the Mátape River, 1653;[5] and "San José de Teópare" in the eastern hills, 1676.[6] Franciscans similarly founded "San José de Batepito," visita[7] of Huásabas on the Bavispe River, not long after 1642; and "San José de Chinapa" on the Sonora river, visita of Arizpe, 1648.[8] The most important of these was certainly "San José Mátape," a Jesuit center with a beautiful large church and the first school in the area.

The latter part of the seventeenth century sees the arrival of Jesuit evangelizers whose successful foundations will leave a better documented tribute to St. Joseph. From his arrival in Mexico in 1681 until his death in 1711, Fr. Eusebio Kino pushes the frontier of Christianity from Sonora north into Pimería Alta (including present day southern Arizona), and west into Baja California.[9] He accompanies Atondo y Antillón's 1683 Baja expedition, one of whose ships is the "San José," and in October they encounter unfavorable winds that do not allow them to land on San José Island where

---

[5] ROCA, 244-245. ECKHART, 16. J. A. DONOHUE, *After Kino, Jesuit Missions in Northwestern New Spain 1711-1767*, St. Louis Missouri 1969, 104.

[6] ROCA, 287-289.

[7] ROCA, 208-209. "Visita" literally means "visit" and indicates a chapel or mission within reasonable distance of its principle station.

[8] ROCA, 151-152. ECKHART, 1.

[9] H. E. BOLTON, *The Padre on Horseback*, Chicago 1986.

Indians had already encountered the faith. Kino writes that after Mass with the crew was celebrated "in honor of St. Joseph to be able to reach quickly a good port of refuge, a propitious wind blew from the east and carried us along."[10]

Traveling overland in December, they come upon a fertile valley with abundant water and a large settlement. Kino reports:

> Since morning, when we left our camping ground, we had promised that the best of what we would find we would dedicate to glorious St. Joseph, and consequently we named this valley, plain, watering place and settlement "San José."

Not far beyond, Mission San José Comundú would one day be founded.[11]

Like so many previous expeditions, this one too is abandoned with the declaration that Baja California is "unconquerable."[12] Kino never gives up hope of returning, however, as he diverts his efforts toward Pimería. There he founds the successful mission of "Nuestra Señora de los Dolores" (Our

---

[10] KINO, in E. J. BURRUS, *Kino Reports to Headquarters*, Rome 1954, 32-35.

[11] BURRUS, *Kino Reports*, 64-71. H. E. BOLTON, *Rim of Christendom*, New York 1936, 148-149.

[12] VICARIATO APOSTOLICO DE LA PAZ, *Anuario de la Iglesia de Dios Padre y del Señor Jesucristo que vive en Baja California Sur*, La Paz, Baja California Sur 1984, 18.

Lady of Sorrows), which will serve as his headquarters for the rest of his life. Two days later, on March 15, 1687, he visits an undiscovered settlement to the north and dubs it "San José Imuris,"[13] as if to immediately have Our Lady's newly founded mission accompanied by one dedicated to her husband.

In 1692 Kino named the present day San Pedro River of Arizona, "San José de Terrenate" or "de Quíburi."[14]

When this "Apostle to the Pimas" is then joined by Juan María Salvatierra and Juan Ugarte, the three become the zealous heroes of evangelization in "sterile and backward" Lower California.[15] In 1697 they achieve the permanent foundation of "Nuestra Señora de Loreto" Mission, the "Mother and Cradle of the Californias."[16] Again Our Lady will be followed by St. Joseph, with the 1701

---

[13] H. H. BANCROFT, *History of the North Mexican States*, San Francisco 1884, I,252-253. ROCA, 56-57. ECKHART, 13. KINO in BOLTON, *Kino's Historical Memoir of Pimería Alta*, Berkeley Calif. 1948, I,111-113, II,239. BOLTON, *Spanish Exploration in the Southwest 1542-1706*, New York 1916, 440.

[14] W. C. BARNES, *Arizona Place Names*, Tucson 1960, 50-51. BOLTON, *Span. Explor. in the SW*, 447,453.

[15] L. N. GARCIA, *Don José de Gálvez y la Concordancia General de las Provincias Internas del Norte de Nueva España*, Sevilla 1964, 44-45. J. J. BAEGERT, *Noticias de la Península Americana de California*, México 1942, 3.

[16] ROBERTSON, 15-19. A. TRASVIÑA-TAYLOR, *Loreto, Madre y Cuna de las Californias*.

founding of "San José de la Laguna," or "San José de Guaymas," on the Guaymas bay estuary as a shipping base to supply California from Sonora.[17]

Earlier that year in an expedition north of Guaymas seeking a land route to California, Salvatierra records in his journal that they began early March 19, 1701, trusting in the protection of St. Joseph. The discovery of two watering places brought them all great joy at being blessed by the Holy Spouse of Mary. They named the stop "San José de Ramos" since the following morning was Palm Sunday.[18]

To the north, near present day Nogales, Arizona, Kino reports a November 4, 1701, overnight stay at "San Joseph de Guevavi," though the name is soon changed.[19] He also established its visita, San Cayetano, which at least since 1773 has been known as "San José de Tumacácori."[20]

Early 1708 sees the founding of mission "San José Comundú" in Baja, named in honor of José de

---

[17]BOLTON, *Rim of Christendom*, 462-463,526-529. BANCROFT, *History of the North Mexican States*, I,511,554. GARCIA, 45,396. DONOHUE, 127,134-135.

[18]BURRUS, *Kino and Manje, Explorers of Sonora and Arizona*, St. Louis Missouri 1971, 608-609,611,613.

[19]BOLTON, *Kino's Hist. Mem. of Pimería Alta*, 307. F. JACKSON SMITH, *Father Kino in Arizona*, Arizona 1966, 91.

[20]J. J. WAGONER, *Early Arizona*, Tucson 1975, 86. BARNES, 326-327.

Villapuente who provided the funds. By the early 1740s a large three nave church was built there.[21]

Mexican Jesuit Clemente Guillén mentions "San José Adagué" where he celebrated Mass on March 19 in his 1719 expedition across the peninsula to Magdalena Bay.[22] A later report of his speaks of the "San José River" in the cape, named for this most holy patriarch because it was discovered on his feast day, March 19, 1725. Guillén calls the territory "San José," and petitions establishment of a mission there.[23] Fathers Tamaral and Echeverría arrived in La Paz for March 19, 1730, and chose the sight for mission "San José del Cabo" or "San José de los Coras," also named in honor of benefactor José de Villapuente.[24] Tamaral's December report already speaks of rapid conversions there and a devotional life that included daily singing of the "Alabado,"[25] presumably with its stanza to St. Joseph, which we will quote later. In the 1734 uprising, Fr. Carranco

[21] P. MARTINEZ, *Historia de Baja California*, México 1956, 64,252-253. BANCROFT, *Hist. of the North Mex. States and Texas*, II,424-425. ALEGRE, 216. L. SALES, *Noticias de las Californias*, Madrid 1960, 83.

[22] W. M. MATHES, *Clemente Guillén, Explorer of the South*, Los Angeles 1979, 44.

[23] C. GUILLEN, "Report 3, from Loreto," in BURRUS, *Jesuit Relations, Baja California 1716-1762*, Los Angeles 1984, 101-103.

[24] MARTINEZ, 212.

[25] N. TAMARAL, "Report 9, from San José de los Coras", in BURRUS, *Jesuit Relations*, 151.

was martyred at nearby Santiago, with the words "Jesus, Mary and Joseph" on his lips.[26] In the subsequent Franciscan period, we will see mention of St. Joseph's image driving away locusts at San José.

San Ignacio, the best preserved Baja mission,[27] has a series of sanctuary paintings including a beautiful large painting of St. Joseph, who is supported by angels, lily in right hand and the child Jesus with cross in left arm. Local people and Fr. Primo Bentivoglio, long-time pastor there, believe it is most probably an original from the eighteenth century.

Also to be mentioned in Sonora are eighteenth century "San José de Soyopa" above the Yaqui River,[28] and "San José de la Gracia" on the Sonora River.[29]

Almost forgotten is the fact that pre-Arizona Tucson was originally christened "San José" on March 19, 1762, as documented in Elias' report: "I applied the name of Señor San José to Tucson, because ... the settlement occurred on the feast of

---

[26]GARCIA, 87. VICARIATO DE LA PAZ, *Anuario 1984*, 8-9. BURRUS, *Jesuit Relations*, 97,149. BANCROFT, *Hist. of North Mex. States*, II,451-456. MARTINEZ, 218

[27]ROBERTSON, 34-36. A. QUARTUCCIO, *Rambling through Baja California with Pen and Brush*, San José California 1984, 62-64.

[28]ROCA, 255-256.

[29]ROCA, 171.

the Holy Patriarch."[30] The name was lost as the church begun there ten years later was dedicated to St. Augustine. It seems though that a chapel constructed in the general vicinity in the 1790s was called "San José."[31]

In 1775 Fr. Francisco Garcés refers to the Estrella Mountains of Arizona as "Sierra de San Joseph de Cumars."[32]

In Jesuit evangelization from the Cape of Baja California to northernmost Pimería, St. Joseph is never absent.

New Mexico

Preliminary Franciscan evangelization campaigns began by 1598. In the winter of 1621-1622 Fray Jerónimo Salmerón founded what some consider the first mission, named "San José de Giusewa" in the area of Jémez. A church there seems either to be completed or under construction in 1626, though surely abandoned by 1658. Since at least 1892, its

---

[30] H. F. DOBYNS, *Spanish Colonial Tucson*, Tucson 1976, 20-21. J. E. OFFICER, *Hispanic Arizona 1536-1856*, Tucson 1987, 7,40,318,340.

[31] DOBYNS, 33,41-42. WAGONER, 113.

[32] BARNES, 294.

great ruins at Giusewa were mistaken for those of San Diego, but today the error has been corrected.[33]

Salmerón also visited Ácoma in 1621. In 1629 Fray Juan Ramírez arrived and presumably began what became a noteworthy church, that in 1672 was called one of the best in the kingdom. A St. Joseph painting hanging there today is said to have been a gift from King Charles II of Spain to Fray Miranda who brought it there in 1629, though I have been unable to substantiate this legend. What is certain is that the image has long been regarded as miraculously capable of producing rain during droughts and of protecting against pestilence, illness and attack, so much so that the mid-nineteenth century witnessed a civil court decision in favor of Ácoma against the Laguna pueblo who had taken possession of it during a drought.[34]

In 1699 a St. Joseph statue was brought from Mexico and dipped into a river in the Laguna area to name it the "San José River," and on July 4 the

---

[33] F. A. DOMÍNGUEZ, in E. B. ADAMS and A. CHÁVEZ, *The Missions of New Mexico, 1776*, Albuquerque N.M. 1956, 189. G. KUBLER, *The Religious Architecture of New Mexico*, Colorado Springs 1940, 16,81-83. E. L. HEWETT, *Handbooks of Archaeological History*, Albuquerque 1943, 83,230.

[34] ADAMS, 189-190. E. R. FORREST, *Missions and Pueblos of the Old Southwest*, Rio Grande Press, 161-164. *THE NEW MEXICO REGISTER, Gallup Cathedral Dedication special supplement*, Gallup N.M. 6/17/1955, 14-15,18. W. CATHER, *Death Comes for the Archbishop*, New York 1971, 88,107. C. HALLENBECK, *Spanish Missions of the Old Southwest*, Garden City N.Y. 1926, 142-143.

pueblo was formally established as "San José de la Laguna." In response to the people's petition, Fray Antonio de Miranda arrived and immediately began construction of a mission church which was quickly readied for Mass, though probably not completed until about 1706. Built of stone, it is today possibly the best preserved of all the old Spanish missions. What is probably the original statue is still extant and used in processions to this day for the great celebration of St. Joseph's feast on September 19, when the weather is better than in March. Fray Domínguez' 1776 description speaks of a large oil painting on canvas given by the king and hanging on the center wall, but it has not been verified if it is present today or could be the one hanging in Ácoma. He also mentions a large oil of St. Joseph on animal skin hanging in the sacristy, which must be one of the two ancient hide paintings still in the mission. Today one is near the altar. Another with St. Joseph and child, done by an early friar and known as one of the largest hide paintings anywhere, hangs to the left of the altar.[35]

---

[35]DOMÍNGUEZ in ADAMS, 182-188. *NEW MEXICO REGISTER*, June 17, 1955 supplement, 16-17. O. FELLIN, *Yahweh, the Voice that Beautifies the Land*, Gallup 1976, 10-11. L. B. PRINCE, *Spanish Mission Churches of New Mexico*, Cedar Rapids Iowa 1915.

Bishop Tamarón visited Trampas of the Picurís and, at the petition of the settlers, issued a decree on June 15, 1760 to build a chapel there "with the title and advocation of Señor San José de la Gracia y de la Santísima María Inmaculada." In 1776 Domínguez relates that the altar is furnished with a board niche containing a middle-sized statue of St. Joseph. After giving credit to Vicar Roybal for his donations, he states: "The rest at the expense of the alms of the Holy Patriarch."[36] A famous mission church remains there today.

Besides missions and images in honor of St. Joseph, devotion to him is also evidenced in eighteenth century New Mexico by observance of the nineteenth day of each month. Domínguez lists among the devotions at La Cañada: "The nineteenth of each month, sung Mass in honor of Lord St. Joseph, at which very many take communion."[37] Here too the patron of the Church brings people to Christ.

Texas

In 1683 in the El Paso area Governor Gironza founded a short-lived presidio and pueblo named

---

[36]DOMÍNGUEZ in ADAMS, 99-101,250-251.
[37]DOMÍNGUEZ in ADAMS, 80.

"Nuestra Señora del Pilar y San José." Luis Navarro García mistakenly presumes that a mission also exists there.[38]

In 1684 the Mendoza expedition from the southwest of El Paso also gave the name "San Joseph" to a gorge with water, wood and pasture.[39]

A Mission to "El Señor San José" is attempted in the same La Junta area in 1715, but has very limited success due to the 1726 Indian uprising.[40]

The lasting story of St. Joseph in Texas, however, is tied to Fr. Antonio Margil, the great Franciscan evangelizer who worked indefatigably from Costa Rica to Texas, and was declared "Venerable" on July 31, 1836.[41] He worked in Texas for only five years, 1716-1722, but in that time pioneered the great missionary effort that was to continue, and founded the great San José Mission. A particular devotion he introduced in all the missions he founded was the singing of the seven stanzas of the "Alabado." After honoring the Blessed Sacrament

[38] GARCIA, 26. D. H. TIMMONS of University of Texas at El Paso, letter to author, March 11, 1989.

[39] BOLTON, *Span. Explor. in the SW*, 333-334.

[40] ECKHART, "Spanish Missions of Texas 1680-1800," in *KIVA*, Arizona February 1967, 4-7,17.

[41] A. G. CICOGNANI, *Santità in America*, New York 1948, 119. M. A. HABIG, *San Antonio's Mission San José*, Chicago 1968, 22.

and the Immaculate Virgin, stanzas three and four
refer to St. Joseph:

> *Y el glorioso San José*
> *Electo por Dios inmenso*
> *Para padre estimativo*
> *De su Hijo, el divino Verbo.*
>
> *Y esto por todos los siglos*
> *Y de los siglos. Amén.*
> *Amén. Jesús y María;*
> *Jesús, María y José.*

A poetic translation of this reads:

> Honor Joseph, spouse of Mary,
> The chosen of God in heaven,
> To his paternal arms so tender
> The Incarnate Son was given.
>
> And so for endless ages
> Shall it be for evermore.
> Amen. Jesus and Mary;
> Jesus, Mary and Joseph.

Joseph is to be praised for all eternity since he was
chosen by God to be a sharer in the Incarnation.

Ven. Margil had this sung after Mass, and a second time at the end of work days after the missionary's instruction.[42]

The Ramón expedition for formal occupancy of Texas in 1716 was accompanied by Margil with friars of Zacatecas, and by other Franciscans from Querétaro. One of the missions immediately founded in eastern Texas was "San José de los Nasonis," near the north line of Nacogdoches County. Unstable times led to its being moved several times. In 1731 it was renamed "San Juan Capistrano," probably due to its nearness to "San José de Aguayo."[43]

St. Joseph's name was to endure on what would be known as the "Queen of the Texas Missions" and even "the best in the hemisphere."[44] Fr. Margil's letter of December 26, 1719, to the newly appointed governor, the Marquis of Aguayo, requests the founding of this mission on an excellent site along the San Antonio River which will be the central hub for branching out in both directions. He

[42] CICOGNANI, 116. HABIG, 195,202.

[43] J. A. MORFI, *History of Texas 1673-1779*, Albuquerque 1935, 185-187,212-213. BANCROFT, *Hist. of North Mex. States*, I,632-633. C. E. CASTAÑEDA, *The Mission Era: The Winning of Texas 1693-1731*, New York 1976, II,60-61,154-155,238-241.

[44] J. M. DAY, "San José", in AA.VV., *Six Missions of Texas*, Waco Texas 1965, 129,143. HABIG, 65-66,233-234. HALLENBECK, 52.

states that he already has sufficient supplies, including:[45]

> a statue of St. Joseph, which had been given to him by Captain Gaspar Larrañaga at the time of his death in Zacatecas, with the request that it be used for the founding of a mission under the advocation of San José.

He diplomatically suggests that it be called "San José y San Miguel de Aguayo" and be the first founded in Texas by the governor, whose first name was José and whose title included "Marquis of San Miguel de Aguayo."

Aguayo's reply of January 22, 1720, orders the foundation under the requested name and charges Margil with the task, which he formally accomplishes on February 23.[46] The mission flourishes despite setbacks, and our patron's feast, March 19, 1768 (not May 19 as mistakenly reported by Juan Agustín Morfi), saw the blessing of the foundation of the new stone church.[47] Fr. Morfi, Texas' first historian, leaves record of his 1777 visit, when construction was nearly completed. He refers to an

[45] MARGIL, in CASTAÑEDA, II,124-126. DAY, 134-135.

[46] CASTAÑEDA, II,126-127. MORFI, 193.

[47] HABIG, 55,61. MORFI, 96. DAY, 146.

image of St. Joseph on its pedestal as one example of the ease with which the stone was worked.[48]

The façade was probably done by the legendary Pedro Huizar and completed around 1790 or later.[49] On the center upper part is a carved statue of St. Joseph, flanked by Sts. Dominic and Francis. On the lower part is Our Lady of Guadalupe, flanked by Sts. Joachim and Anne, each of whom have a heart above their head. These are said to represent the hearts of Joseph and Mary, which formed a trinity with an image of the Sacred Heart below a carved cross that originally crowned the façade.[50]

Inventories list numerous statues of St. Joseph.[51] Statues of Mary and Joseph were carried in procession during the rosary "on Saturdays, the nineteenth of each month, and feasts of Christ and of the Blessed Virgin."[52] We have already mentioned the daily praying of the "Alabado."

---

[48] MORFI, 97.

[49] J. W. BURKE, *A Forgotten Glory*, Waco 1979, 101-104. DAY, 150-151.

[50] DAY, 150. HABIG, 234.

[51] SR. M. R. WARBURTON, curator of *Old Spanish Missions Historical Research*, San Antonio Texas.

[52] HABIG, *The San José Papers: The Primary Sources for the History of Mission San José y San Miguel de Aguayo from its Founding in 1720 to the Present*, Part I: 1717-1791, San Antonio 1978, 148.

Through all the changes of secularization, Mexican independence, Texas' war of independence, and eventual statehood in the U. S. A., the mission church survives today in a restored form, keeping the name of San José engraved in Texan history.

THE BIRTH OF CHRISTIANITY IN ALTA CALIFORNIA

Though Cabrillo's expedition of 1542 and Vizcaíno's of 1602-1603 gave Spain the right to claim discovery of Upper California, the mid-eighteenth century finds it still without any successful Christian settlements. It remains the last frontier on the northern rim of New Spain. We have seen the background history of the surrounding areas from Baja California to Texas. To really understand St. Joseph's presence in Alta California, however, we must also examine the background of its founder, Junipero Serra, beatified on September 25, 1988.

Blessed Junipero Serra's Background

Serra is a true son of the eighteenth century, born on November 24, 1713, and baptized that same day as Miguel *Joseph*. Fr. Francisco Palóu, his biographer and lifelong friend, states that he kept these names for his confirmation in 1715, but the parish archive in Serra's native Petra of Mallorca, omits Joseph, listing only Miguel.[53] Though known to posterity as Junipero, the name taken at his religious profession,[54] he never ceased to trust in St. Joseph's patronage, received with the middle name given him at birth. Record of his priestly ordination has not been preserved, but he was given faculties to preach on the significant date of March 19, 1738.[55]

After years as a professor, the opportunity arrived in 1749 to join the missionary efforts of the Franciscans in Mexico City. Departure was quick, but not before a good-bye visit to his hometown of Petra. He was there Easter Tuesday when special festivities were held at the shrine of "Mare de Déu de Bon Any" (Mother of God of the Good Year). No one from Petra would leave Mallorca without asking Our Lady's blessing. Like any devout person, he would not miss the procession that day up the hill to her shrine. The people would gather early in

[53] M. GEIGER, *Palóu's Life of Fray Junípero Serra*, Washington D.C. 1955, 3,316-317. *IUNIPERI SERRA POSITIO SUPER VITA ET VIRTUTIBUS*, 90, Vatican City 1981, 21-22.

[54] D. DeNEVI and N. F. MOHOLY, *Junipero Serra*, San Francisco 1985, 16-18.

[55] *POSITIO*, 26.

the morning and march together along with a highly venerated local statue of St. Joseph, carried on the shoulders of four men, and a relic of St. Joseph borne by the vested celebrant. On arrival at the top, the statue and relic of St. Joseph would be placed in the niche with the statue of Our Lady of Bon Any. The day closed in the church below with seven recitations of the Lord's Prayer in honor of St. Joseph, and distribution of blessed bay leaves to be placed in their fields for an abundant harvest through the intercession of Mary and Joseph.[56]

In the boat trip from Mallorca, Serra found his life threatened by a hostile English skipper. He safely survived this first stage of his lifelong missionary activity, to dock in Málaga, Spain on Sunday, April 27, 1749, the Feast of the Patronage of St. Joseph.[57] Though not in the universal Church calendar until 1847, this feast of the third Sunday of Easter had been in the calendar of the Diocese of México since 1703 and in that of all Franciscans since 1733.[58]

---

[56] GEIGER, *The Life and Times of Fray Junípero Serra*, O.F.M., Washington D.C. 1969, I,45-47. DeNEVI, 28.

[57] GEIGER, *Palóu's Life*, 12-13,331 (mistakenly calculating April 28 in footnote). GEIGER, *Life and Times*, I,52. DeNEVI, 31.

[58] T. STRAMARE, *San Giuseppe, Virgulto Rigoglioso*, Casale Monferrato AL Italy 1987, 81.

Having safely crossed the Atlantic, Junipero set out on foot from Veracruz towards Mexico City without money or guide, his breviaries and his trust in divine providence being his sole possessions. This trust is not betrayed in this first of many journeys in the New World. A man appeared several times during the journey to help Serra and his companion ford a stream, to offer shelter late on a wet freezing night, to provide pomegranates that slake their thirst on one occasion and bread to give them strength on another. Palóu tells us:

> At various times, the Venerable Father Junípero mentioned these events in order to exhort his hearers to trust in divine Providence. He said that the benefactor was either the Patriarch St. Joseph or some devout man whose heart this Saint touched to do these acts of charity towards them.[59]

Palóu notes that in Serra's catechesis of the Pame and Otomí in the Sierra Gorda, he also promoted the devotion to the saints, listing the Most Holy Patriarch St. Joseph immediately after Michael the Archangel, and before their own Se-

---

[59]GEIGER, *Palóu's Life*, 17-19,337. *POSITIO*, 372-373. GEIGER, *Life and Times*, I,83-86.

raphic Father St. Francis.[60] Among the devotions he taught was also the "Alabado" with its inclusion of St. Joseph, as we saw earlier.[61]

Since his first assignment in America in 1749, Junipero had been based at San Fernando College, from where he would depart to preach missions throughout the various dioceses of Mexico. Another episode out of the ordinary took place sometime between September, 1758, and July, 1767, as he was returning to the college after preaching a mission in La Huasteca. He and his companions were preparing to sleep in the open one night when they suddenly spotted a house nearby. The couple inside with child graciously fed and lodged them. Continuing their journey in the morning, they soon came upon some muleteers who assure them that there was no house at all anywhere in that area. Palóu relates the reaction of Serra and his companions:

> The missionaries then believed that it had been divine Providence which had granted them the favor of that hospitality, and that undoubtedly those persons who were within the house were Jesus, Mary and Joseph. They

---

[60] GEIGER, *Palóu's Life*, 31. *POSITIO*, 67,377.
[61] GEIGER, *Life and Times*, I,166-167. GEIGER, *Palóu's Life*, 29,31,346-347.

pondered not only the neatness and cleanliness of the house, despite its poverty, and the affectionate tenderness with which they dispensed their hospitality, but also the extraordinary inner consolation which they had felt in their hearts there.[62]

Baja and the Expedition to Alta California

In mid 1767 the background of St. Joseph's general presence in the northwestern rim of New Spain merges with the background of his particular presence in the personal life of Blessed Junipero Serra. Less than a month after the Jesuits are expelled, Serra is named president of the Baja California missions they leave behind. Arriving there with fourteen companions on April 1, 1768, he immediately sets out to visit and to assign priests to the missions, including the missions of San José de Comundú and San José del Cabo.

By May of 1768, however, José de Gálvez, the Visitor General of New Spain, received news of Russian movements in the Aleutian Islands and rushed to San Blas on the coast of Sonora to plan for the occupation of Upper California. Gálvez

---

[62] GEIGER, *Palóu's Life*, 45-46. DeNEVI, 60-61. BANCROFT, *History of California*, San Francisco 1886, I,414. Popularized in CATHER, 279-282.

himself, being a former acolyte and seminarian, and bearing the name "Joseph," was also to be instrumental in bringing St. Joseph's patronage to Alta California.[63] While at San Blas, he was able to inspect and approve the first naval vessel built there, a packet boat that would be christened the "San José" in honor of his most holy patriarch.[64]

Before Serra could get the missionary work well established in Baja, Gálvez was already making plans with him for the expedition to Alta California. The two agreed on policies for the missions, the fair treatment of the Indians, the sharing of church goods from the Baja missions, and on St. Joseph's patronage. Regarding the church goods, Serra inventories the property already collected by Gálvez, which in Palóu's listing includes "one box containing statues of Jesus, Mary and Joseph."[65] He himself completes the initial allocation the following year as itemized in a letter to Palóu, including eight medium-sized prints of the mysteries of Most

---

[63] H. I. PRIESTLY, *José de Gálvez*, Berkeley 1916, 2-3. K. and E. AINSWORTH, *In the Shade of the Juniper Tree*, Garden City N.Y. 1970, 28-29.

[64] R. BRANDES, "Patron Ship of Sacred Expedition," in F. J. WEBER, *Some Reminiscences about Fray Junípero Serra*, Santa Barbara Calif. 1985, 25-28.

[65] BANCROFT, *Hist. of Calif.*, I,118-119. AINSWORTH, 116.

Holy Mary and St. Joseph, from the church in Loreto.[66]

Of particular interest is the place of St. Joseph in the naming of the new missions and in the patronage of the expedition. Serra's letter of August 24, 1768, has not been preserved, but we do have Gálvez' September 15 reply to him, which could very well be understood as an answer to his request that St. Francis and St. Joseph be included in the naming. Gálvez notes that the names of San Diego, San Francisco and Monterey are to be retained as given by previous expeditions. Subsequent missions can be named after St. Bonaventure and other Franciscan saints. The mission at Monterey is to be "San Carlos" in honor of King Charles III of Spain, and Viceroy Carlos de Croix of New Spain. The church at Monterey, however, is to bear the title of "St. Joseph," the patron of the expedition and of Gálvez himself. The humble saint will not mind sharing the honors with St. Charles:

> My patron will not be offended in that we circumscribe his honor by limiting the title to the church, for he was very humble and through many centuries of Christianity his name has been given to the poor who are

---

[66] A. TIBESAR, *Writings of Junípero Serra*, Washington D.C. 1955, I,124-125.

born to be artisans. Moreover, he already has two missions on the peninsula [San José de Comundú and San José del Cabo] entrusted to him so that he may protect all present and future missions.[67]

Serra notes in his Diary that on September 28 he "sang a votive Mass at Loreto in honor of St. Joseph, who was elected patron of both the sea and land expeditions."[68] In October Serra is visiting the southernmost missions including San José del Cabo.[69]

Gálvez' official decree naming St. Joseph patron of the expedition is dated November 21, 1768. He gives two reasons for trusting in the saint's intercession: his incomparable dignity as the reputed father of Christ, and the effectiveness the previous year, 1767, of bringing his image into the fields near San José del Cabo to ward off the swarms of locusts. He charges the missionaries not only to solemnly celebrate St. Joseph's feast each year, but also to offer a solemn Mass and litany in his honor on the nineteenth of every month, imploring divine protection through his intercession. The last part of this

---

[67] GEIGER, *Life and Times*, I,205. GEIGER, *Palóu's Life*, 370,385.

[68] TIBESAR, 40-41. *IUNIPERI SERRA RELATIO ET VOTA*, Vatican City 1983, 129.

[69] GEIGER, *Palóu's Life*, 375.

document found in the Santa Barbara Archives reads as follows:[70]

> Last year when the natives of San Joseph del Cabo saw the threat of losing their poor cornfields to clouds of locusts which were falling upon them, with fervent devotion they brought to the fields the patron image of the Holy Patriarch. The present expeditions to the famous port of Monterrey are undertaken in the confidence that they will be protected by the same patron saint. I ask and entrust to the Reverend Fathers of all the missions, that in addition to the *Salve* which is sung on Saturday each week to Our Most Holy Lady of Loreto, Patroness of all the conversions of the Californias, they

---

[70] *"Desde el año próximo anterior en que los naturales de San Joseph del Cabo, viéndose amenazados de perder sus pobres milpas por las nubes de langostas que caían sobre ellas, sacaron a los campos con fervorosa devoción la imagen tutelar del Santo Patriarca y que las actuales expediciones al famoso Puerto de Monterrey se emprenden en la confianza de que serán patrocinadas por el mismo santo: ruego y encargo a los Reverendísimos Padres Ministros de todas las Misiones, que además de la salve que en los sábados de cada semana se canta a María Santísima de Loreto, Patrona de todas las conversiones de Californias, y de celebrar perpetuamente la fiesta solemne y votiva de su santo esposo en el día propio que le tiene dedicado la iglesia católica para se liberte de langosta toda la Península, canten una misa el diez y nueve de cada mes, y la letanía de rogativa mientras duraren los dos viajes de mar y tierra, implorando por medio de la intercesión del glorioso Patriarca el auxilio divino para que ambos tengan el deseado buen suceso, y se consiga fijar para siempre el estandarte sacrosanto de la Cruz de Cristo en medio de la numerosa gentilidad que ocupa los países del Norte de esta dilatada Provincia."* J. DE GÁLVEZ, La Paz Nov. 21, 1768, Document 39a, Santa Barbara Archives, 3-4; thanks to FRS. F. GUEST and V. BIASOL, O.F.M. for access to the Spanish transcription in the archives. BANCROFT, *Hist. of Calif.*, I,119. GEIGER, *Palóu's Life*, 56,371.

perpetually celebrate the solemn and votive feast of her holy spouse on the proper day that the Catholic Church has dedicated to him, in order to free the whole peninsula of locusts; that they sing a Mass the nineteenth of each month as well as the prayerful litany for the duration of the sea and land expeditions, imploring through the intercession of the glorious Patriarch the divine help that both may meet with the desired success, and that they succeed in bringing the most holy banner of the Cross of Christ into the midst of the numerous peoples that occupy the countries to the North of this vast province. One author comments: "as well would they have gone without sails as without the holy protector."[71]

Preparations were hastened and Fr. Serra celebrated Mass in honor of the most holy Patriarch St. Joseph on January 9, 1769, to bless the first sea expedition departing from La Paz on the "San Carlos."[72] Similarly on February 15 a Mass was

---

[71] R. D. HUNT, *California and the Californians*, San Francisco 1926, I,156.
[72] *POSITIO*, 385. GEIGER, *Palóu's Life*, 56,371.

sung in honor of St. Joseph to launch the second sea expedition aboard the "San Antonio."[73]

The first land expedition of Captain Rivera and Fr. Crespí left Velicatá on Good Friday, March 24, 1769. Serra was to accompany Governor Portolá on the other land expedition, but convinced him rather to go ahead on his own. Serra's foot and leg were so swollen and infected that Portolá believed it truly impossible for him to make the journey; Gálvez also tried to dissuade him; and Palóu wept. Blessed Junipero unflinchingly asserted that he would never turn back and that he trusted that God's providence would bring him to San Diego and Monterey. He zealously set out from Loreto on March 28, visited San José de Comundú on April 2, and caught up with Portolá at Velicatá by May 13.[74]

Gálvez had thus succeeded in dispatching four divisions, but he had problems with the new packet boat *San José*, named for the patron of the expedition. On May 1, 1769, he finally had the ship blessed by Palóu and formally named in honor of his most holy patriarch St. Joseph. The problems of the patron ship did not cease, however, and it was

[73]GEIGER, *Palóu's Life*, 57. F. PALOU, *Relación Histórica de la Vida y Apostólicas Tareas del Venerable Padre Fray Junípero Serra*, México 1787, 61.

[74]GEIGER, *Palóu's Life*, 57. DeNEVI, 73-81. SERRA, *Diary*, in *RELATIO* 130-140. BANCROFT, *Hist. of Calif.*, I,121-123.

eventually lost at sea with captain, crew and cargo never to be seen again.[75]

The entry under July 1, 1769, in Serra's diary of his nine hundred mile journey from Loreto reads: "Puerto de San Diego, Gracias a Dios." The four expeditions are successfully reunited. The diary ends as follows:

> Sunday, the second, Feast of the visitation of Our Lady, we sang a Mass to thank her Most Holy Spouse, Patron of both expeditions of sea and land, seeing all their parts now reunited into one in this their immediate destination.[76]

On July 15 another sung Mass in honor of St. Joseph was offered, this time to begin Portolá's overland journey in search of Monterey.[77] Crespí was chaplain and diarist. Serra stayed to found Mission San Diego. The going was rough for Portolá and Crespí. By September 20, they are faced with what appears an endless sea of mountains; severe cold is approaching; some of the men are disabled by scurvy. It is their "unfailing confidence in their

---

[75] BRANDES, in WEBER, 29-35. BANCROFT, *Hist. of Calif.*, I,123.

[76] TIBESAR, I,120-123. BANCROFT, *Hist. of Calif.*, I,136.

[77] PALOU, 81. GEIGER, *Palóu's Life*, 75. DeNEVI, 92-93.

great patron St. Joseph" that allows them to press on bravely.[78]

St. Joseph, the patron who inspired them to undertake this expedition will also inspire the trust for them to see the mission through to its completion.

March 19, 1770 — St. Joseph Saves the Expedition

The greatest challenge to the Spaniards' perseverance came in early 1770, after Portolá and Crespí rejoined Serra in San Diego, having spotted San Francisco Bay, but without finding Monterey. Food supplies grew perilously low. By the beginning of March, Portolá's men were anxious to return. Serra was determined to stay no matter what. It had been 166 years since the early expedition, and he feared that abandonment now would stifle efforts for another century or so. He convinced all to pray a novena to the expedition's patron, and to wait at least until his feast on March 19.[79]

On the day of the deadline, the men were already prepared for the return journey, as Serra

[78]BANCROFT, *Hist. of Calif.*, I,149.

[79]*POSITIO*, 124-125. GEIGER, *Life and Times*, I,239-241. GEIGER, *Palóu's Life*, 80-87. F. B. COMPANYS, *Gaspar de Portolá*, Lerida 1983, 322-323.

sang and preached the St. Joseph Mass. It was mid-afternoon of the very day of March 19 when the sails of the *San Antonio* were seen on the horizon heading for Monterey. The ship lost an anchor in the Santa Bárbara Channel where Indians notified the crew that their companions had returned to San Diego. Within four days the much needed supplies reached the mission.[80]

There is no doubt whatsoever that this event called a last minute halt to the programmed abandonment of Upper California. It has been stated: "The establishment of the colony of New California may be said to date from Monday, March 19, 1770."[81] Serra himself begins an April 16 letter with this simple fact: "Since the *San Antonio* ... arrived at this port on the Feast of St. Joseph, ... the officers in command here decided on a second trip to Monterey."[82] Palóu writes in *Noticias*:

> There is no doubt that [abandonment] would have occurred if God had not ordered that on the very day of San José, to whose patronage the event was attributed, as he is

---

[80] I. ENGSTRAND, "Founding Father of San Diego," in WEBER, 49. K. M. KING, *Mission to Paradise*, Chicago 1975, 45-48.
[81] O. ENGLEBERT, *Adventurer Saints*, New York 1956, 234.
[82] TIBESAR, I,162-163.

patron of the expeditions and the new reduc-
tions, a sail should appear...[83]

In his biography of Serra he declares:

The men attributed it to a miracle through
the intercession of the Holy Patriarch that
on his very feast day, the day the expedition
had set as the term of its stay, the ship was
descried...[84]

Additional documentation amply supports the
attribution of the event to the miraculous interces-
sion of St. Joseph. The diary entry of an eyewitness,
Fr. Crespí, for March 25 or later, relates: "Blessed
St. Joseph placed [the ship] before our eyes."[85]
Portolá likewise writes to DeCroix on April 17:

... taking into account the fact that it arrived
in the vicinity of this port the day of St. Joseph, our patron for this expedition, ... I
firmly believe that the Saint intervened so
that it interrupt its voyage to Monterey...[86]

On August 2 Armona, governor of Baja California,
writes to México summarizing the news he received:

---

[83] PALOU, in BOLTON, *Historical Memoirs of New California*, Berkeley Calif.
1926, II,273-274.

[84] PALOU, in GEIGER, *Palóu's Life*, 87; in *POSITIO*, 395.

[85] J. CRESPI, in *POSITIO*, 153; there is also a copy in the Santa Barbara
Archives, document 208.

[86] PORTOLA, in Santa Barbara Archives, Document 210; also in GEIGER,
Palóu's Life, 388.

> On the day of March 19 from San Diego
> Mission there was sighted the Packet boat
> San Antonio, also known as the Prince. This
> brought great joy to all the members of the
> land expedition who had decided to wait
> until the nineteenth, said day of Lord St.
> Joseph. It seems that the Holy Patriarch
> wished to detain them with this glimpse of
> help so that they not march for Loreto the
> following day.[87]

Serra thereafter continued to celebrate a most
solemn Mass in honor of St. Joseph on the nineteenth of every month until his death.[88] The results
of this novena have been cited as "the closest we get
to the supernatural in Serra's life."[89] Palóu recalls
the event twice in his final chapter on Serra's
virtues, as an outstanding example of his fortitude
and his faith: "He remained calm in adversity,
placing his trust in God."[90] Serra's faith and fortitude were rewarded through St. Joseph's intercession in a way that could hardly be called coincid-

---

[87] M. ARMONA, in Santa Barbara Archives, Document 226; also in GEIGER, *Palóu's Life,* 388.

[88] PALOU, *Relación Histórica,* 97. DeNEVI, 97.

[89] T. MAYNARD, *The Long Road of Father Serra,* London 1956, 271-272.

[90] *"Non adverso perturbatur." "In adversis in Deo confidit."* PALOU, in GEIGER, *Palóu's Life,* 275-276,283; in *POSITIO,* 448,454.

ence. The expedition was saved, and the virginal
father of the Savior born at Bethlehem can rightly
be called "Father of the birth of Christianity in Alta
California."

The Remainder of Blessed Serra's Life

St. Joseph would continue to be present to Serra
the rest of his days and would guide the expedition
entrusted to him all the way to its completion.
Once the supplies arrived, no time was wasted in
returning to find Monterey. On Pentecost Sunday,
June 3, 1770, Serra celebrated the founding Mass
for the Carmel Mission, under the same oak tree
where the first California Mass had been celebrated
by Carmelite missionaries back in 1602. The new
church where Serra would one day be buried was to
be under the patronage of St. Joseph, though the
mission would be called San Carlos Borromeo, in
accord with Gálvez' decree we saw earlier [p. 36].
Included in the prayers after Mass were devotions
to the Trinity, Mary, "Most Holy St. Joseph, patron
of the expedition" and St. Charles.[91] Gálvez do-
nated a statue of St. Joseph for the mission which
can still be seen there today, although the original

---

[91] SERRA to Andrés, June 12, 1770, in TIBESAR, I,168-169; in *RELATIO*, 176-177. PALOU, in BOLTON, *Memoirs*, II,294. BANCROFT, *Hist. of Calif.*, I,170-171. GEIGER, *Life and Times*, I,247. DeNEVI, 100-101.

child, lily-staff, and silver halo have been lost. It is listed among the gifts of the King at the time of the founding. Serra's 1774 Report says that during the past year a 5½ foot wide niche with redwood cupola was built for it. The statue is mid-eighteenth century Mexico, polychrome estofado.[92]

Serra's first recorded baptism in Upper California is registered in Carmel December 26, 1770 after the initials: "*V^a. Jhs. M^a. Jph.*," "Hail Jesus, Mary and Joseph."[93] Baptism number 15 in this register takes place on St. Joseph's feast, March 19 of the following year. The one baptized was "Juan Joseph," whom Serra would take with him to Mexico City to have confirmed there in 1773. He was the first native to be confirmed, and the viceroy looked on him as the first fruits of evangelization.[94] Subsequent confirmations would be performed by Serra himself, beginning on June 29, 1778 in Monterey at

---

[92] BOLTON, *Font's Complete Diary*, Berkeley 1931, 290-291. TIBESAR, II,242-243. N. NEUERBURG, "Mission Churches in Serra's Time," in WEBER, 71. M. MORGADO, *Legacy of Junípero Serra*, Pacific Grove Calif. 1987. R. J. MENN, *Mission San Carlos Borromeo*, Carmel Calif. "Estofado" is a process of finishing sculptures with gilding, punched patterns and paint.

[93] GEIGER, *Palóu's Life*, 392.

[94] GEIGER, *Palóu's Life*, 134,412-413.

the "Mission of the Ichxenta Ranch which we call *St. Joseph.*"[95]

Not only Serra's first baptismal registry, but all his letters and writings throughout his life begin with "Hail Jesus, Mary, Joseph!" He taught this greeting to the Indians, and by August of 1772 he writes that "for great distances the only greeting heard from them is 'Love God. Hail Jesus, Mary and Joseph.'"[96]

On November 1, 1776, Serra founded Mission San Juan Capistrano, a famous tourist attraction today because of the returning migration of swallows every March 19. Popular brochures and guidebooks are quick to assert that this goes back to the time of Serra himself. Mr. Richard Landy, Director of Tourism there, states however that the celebration was probably begun by the pastor who served there 1910-1933, since he was born on March 19. A promotional book by Bill Smith, purporting to be an historian, claims that in 1777, the first St. Joseph Day at the new Mission, a Fr. Fermín Fuster registered the swallows' arrival and continued to do so each subsequent year, as preserved in the mission

---

[95] GEIGER, *Palóu's Life*, 205,450.
[96] SERRA to Verger, August 8, 1772, in TIBESAR, I,256-257; in *RELATIO*, 185. GEIGER, *Life and Times*, I,332.

archives.[97] Archivist Charles Bodnar shows this is simply not true. First of all, the entries are not to be found. Secondly, there was no Fr. Fermín at the Mission, though a Fr. Vicente Fuster came in November of 1779. Fr. Serra was never at Capistrano in March, but only October-November of 1776 and October of 1778 and 1783.[98]

For 1782 two of Serra's St. Joseph Masses are recorded. On March 19 on arrival at Mission San Gabriel, he overlooked his tiredness after his long journey and immediately had the bells rung for the Solemn Mass he sung with a fervent discourse on the Most Holy Patriarch.[99] The following month Serra celebrated his first Mass in the area of Santa Bárbara. It was to bless the ground and raise the cross for the foundation of the presidio. The date was April 21, 1782, Feast of the Patronage of St. Joseph, and Palóu again comments that the homily was fervent. The "Alabado" concluded the function.[100]

No records remain to indicate the contents of Serra's preaching on St. Joseph, but we have some indications of what books may have been available

[97] B. SMITH, *The Swallows of Capistrano*, Riverside Calif., 9-10.
[98] Z. ENGELHARDT, *San Juan Capistrano Mission*, Los Angeles 1922, 228.
[99] PALOU, *Relación*, 245; also in *POSITIO*, 417; in GEIGER, *Palóu's Life*, 220.
[100] GEIGER, *Palóu's Life*, 230,464. DeNEVI, 191.

to him. The first library in California was started by
Serra at Carmel in 1771. One of the books he
brought is Francisco A. Pérez' 1780 translation
from French, *Elogios Históricos de los Santos*, which
has 26 pages commenting on Matthew's "Joseph
her husband was a just man."[101] Another volume in
the library there is the 1785 second edition of
Pedro Díaz de Guereñu's *Año Panegýrico*, whose St.
Joseph day sermon for March fills 29 pages,
commenting on the same verse from Matthew.[102] It
is likely that Serra would have known the first
edition. Richard Joseph Menn, Curator of the San
Carlos Borromeo Mission Library and Archives,
vouches for the fact that devotional tracts and
novena leaflets on St. Joseph dating from Serra's
time were plentiful, but are no longer kept at
Carmel. The missionaries would carry pockets full
of such booklets to give people.[103]

Several pertinent volumes are also to be found in
the Santa Barbara Archives. These include Palóu's
personal copy of Carmelite Juan de San Joseph's
1727 *Sermones Varios de Santos* dedicated to St.
Joseph. The first eighty-six pages of the second

---

[101] *"Joseph vir justus erat"* (Matthew 1:19). F. A. PÉREZ, trans., *Elogios Históricos
de los Santos*, 1780, I,314-339.

[102] P. DÍAZ DE GUEREÑU, *Año Panegýrico*, Madrid 1785, II,114-142.

[103] R. A. CURLETTI, "Los Regalitos de Fray Junípero," in WEBER, 97-102.

volume contain four sermons on St. Joseph to be given to Carmelites in the presence of the Blessed Sacrament exposed. These are preceded by an acrostic poem "O JOSEPH SPONSE REGINAE CAELORUM VIRGINIS."[104] There is also Murcia's 1753 *Clarín Evangélico Panegírico* with nine March sermons on St. Joseph,[105] Torres' 1760 *Año Josephino* with a St. Joseph sermon and prayer for each day of the year,[106] and Joseph Diez' *Aljaba Apostólica* with the complete "Alabado," the Joys of St. Joseph, and songs such as:

> Today, Joseph, with melodious voice
> I will sing your rosy beauty,
> for you were Father of the Sun
> and Husband of the Dawn.[107]

Serra quite possibly would have known the *Vida del Señor San José* by the Mexican Jesuit Vallejo, who published his first edition in 1774 and second edition in 1779.[108]

---

[104] J. DE SAN JOSEPH, *Sermones Varios de Santos*, Pamplona 1727, II,1-86.

[105] J. B. DE MURCIA, *Clarín Evangélico Panegírico*, Barcelona 1753, I, Sermons VII-XV.

[106] I. DE TORRES, *Año Josephino*, México 1760.

[107] *Hoy Joseph, con voz sonora, Cantaré vuestro arrebol, Pues fuisteis Padre del Sol, Y el Esposo de la Aurora.* J. DIEZ, *Aljaba Apostólica*, fourth re-printing México 1785, 86-91,380-384,405-408. GEIGER, *Life and Times*, 166-167.

[108] J. I. VALLEJO, *Vida del Señor San José*, third ed. México 1845.

The close of Blessed Junipero's life was also in the embrace of St. Joseph. After 15 years of faithfully celebrating a solemn Mass on the nineteenth of each month in honor of the expedition's patron who had saved them on March 19, 1770, he asked Fr. Palóu to celebrate it for him on August 19, 1784. Though too weak to celebrate, he did not fail to participate in the singing. He died nine days later.[109] The friar who, when declared unfit for the expedition, had asserted that he would never turn back, traveled enough overland miles throughout North America to circumnavigate the globe.[110] The heroic pioneer of Alta California was accompanied by St. Joseph from his birth to his death. He relied on the patronage of St. Joseph whenever an unfavorable outcome was feared.[111] His trust in Divine Providence was never disappointed.

Alta California

The eighteenth century history of St. Joseph in this furthest corner of New Spain, as well as that of Upper California itself, is largely Serra's story. A few other items remain to be treated, however. The

---

[109] GEIGER, *Palóu's Life*, 243,473. *POSITIO*, 422,479. BANCROFT, *Hist. of Calif.*, I,410. DeNEVI, 201.
[110] DeNEVI, 214.
[111] PALOU, in GEIGER, 287; in *POSITIO*, 458.

first of these is the founding of San José de
Guadalupe. It was California's first town for Spanish civilian settlers, whereas the missions were for
the Indians and the presidios for the soldiers.
Though this took place on November 29, 1777,
Serra had nothing to do with it, since he felt it was
too close to the Santa Clara Mission.[112] The name
was apparently selected by the new governor Neve
in honor of the patron of California and for its
proximity to the Guadalupe River named the
previous year.[113] By 1799 the people sought to have
their own chapel and in 1803 the cornerstone was
laid for San José de Guadalupe Church, the first in
California outside a mission or presidio.[114] A legend
exists here too about the swallows returning for St.
Joseph's Day.[115] In 1849 San José became the first
capital of the State of California.[116]

The other notable honor to St. Joseph comes at
the very end of the eighteenth century, well after

---

[112] DeNEVI, 173-174.

[113] E. A. BEILHARZ, *Felipe de Neve*, San Francisco 1971, 102-103.
BANCROFT, *Hist. of Calif.*, I,312. PALOU, *Relación*, 225. C. ARBUCKLE, *History of
San José*, San José Calif. 1985, 10.

[114] BEILHARZ and D. O. DeMERS, *San José: California's First City*, Tulsa
Oklahoma 1980, 5-6. Thanks to L. MASUNAGA and staff for access to the archives
of the San José Historical Society.

[115] M. B. KAUFMAN, "St. Joseph's was first Pueblo Church," *San José Mercury
News*, January 9, 1966, 12.

[116] E. G. GUDDE, *California Place Names*, Berkeley 1965, 272.

Serra's death. On June 11, 1797, Serra's successor, Fr. Lasuén, founded Mission San José. Originally "Oroysom," it had been christened "San Francisco Solano" for a brief time and then "San Carlos Borromeo" before Viceroy Branciforte issued the decree and Lasuén applied the official title "Misión del gloriosísimo patriarcha Señor San Joseph." It was also known as "San José de Guadalupe" for its proximity to the Guadalupe river flowing through the San José Valley and near the town of San José.[117] Historian Fr. Abeloe, who worked in the modern restoration of the mission, observed: "It seems strange that St. Joseph should have to wait so long for an Alta California mission to bear his name."[118] At the first baptism there on September 2, 1797, a 24 year old woman named Gilpae was given the name "Josefa."[119]

From the mission's nineteenth century history, the following details are worthy of note: the arrival of the central life-size statue of St. Joseph and child

[117] F. F. McCARTHY, *The History of Mission San José California 1797-1835*, Fresno Calif. 1958, 39,45. F. F. DE LASUEN, M. WALSH, R. H. BECKER, in F. J. WEBER, *The Patriarchal Mission*, Hong Kong 1985, 3-8,153,183. BANCROFT, *Hist. of Calif.*, I,555.

[118] W. N. ABELOE, in WEBER, *Patriarchal Mission*, 219.

[119] Ibid. McCARTHY, 59-60.

in 1807;[120] the dedication of the church on the vigil of the patronage of St. Joseph, April 22, 1809;[121] subsequent most solemn annual celebration of St. Joseph's feast;[122] dedication of the bells in honor of St. Joseph;[123] and the 1833 and 1850 inventories listing images of St. Joseph.[124] The St. Joseph statue presently behind the altar is reported as fifteenth century Spanish, and a painting of St. Joseph and child that hung in the museum in the 1980s bore the caption: "Painted in México before 1800."

Of course, St. Joseph's name was most likely present in many other small local settings in Upper California by the end of the eighteenth century. We have already noted Rancho San José Ichxenta [p. 48 above]. Another such example is "Rancho San José de la Gracia de Simí" in the San Fernando area, a grant by Governor Borica around 1795.[125]

We have also spoken of the St. Joseph statue at San Carlos Mission and subsequent St. Joseph images at the San José mission [pp. 46, 54 above].

---

[120] McCARTHY, 119.

[121] McCARTHY, 125-128. ABELOE, in WEBER, 220.

[122] McCARTHY, 128-130. E. B. WEBB, *Indian Life at the Old Missions*, Los Angeles, 264-265.

[123] McCARTHY, 160-167. WALSH, in WEBER, 154-155.

[124] McCARTHY, 123. J. M. REAL and J. NOBILI, in WEBER, 78,80,85.

[125] BANCROFT, *Hist. of Calif.*, I,663.

Eighteenth century inventories, most notably that of 1783, evidence the presence of such images of St. Joseph in virtually every California mission: a life-size painting in Mission San Francisco; another of St. Joseph and the Immaculate Conception at San Diego, as well as the surviving Christ child from a St. Joseph statue destroyed in the 1775 revolt; at Carmel, besides the silver-haloed life-size statue mentioned above, an 18 inch painting of the death of St. Joseph brought from México; a similar such painting at Mission San Antonio; a canvas at San Gabriel; a 1771 request for a St. Joseph painting for San Luis Obispo; and a statue with child on a bracket or pedestal at San Juan Capistrano.[126] Present day holdings at the missions are plentiful and varied, though only rare exceptions are traceable to the origins. The number of St. Joseph images is probably second only to that of St. Francis, the patron of the missionary evangelizers who bear his name.[127]

---

[126]NEURERBURG, in WEBER, *Some Reminiscences*, 67-75. TIBESAR, II, 242-243.

[127]K. BAER, "St. Joseph in California Mission Art," in *St. Joseph Magazine*, St. Benedict Oregon March 1956, 28-33.

Conclusion

St. Joseph was continually present in all of New Spain from the start, including expansion along the northern circumference. His patronage throughout the life of Blessed Junipero Serra, and particularly at the time of the founding of modern Upper California, however, gives him a special right to the title "Father of the Birth of Christianity in Alta California." Serra has been honored in statues, on a postage stamp, and even in the naming of a freeway, while Californians are scarcely aware of the meaning or reason for the name of the city of San José, let alone of the primary patron for the church at Carmel mission and for California itself. Blessed Serra certainly wishes us to remember the credit St. Joseph deserves in our history. In our wealthy and rapidly growing environment of self-reliance, we Californians surely have more need today then ever before to beg Joseph's intercession to recover that trust in divine providence that enabled Fr. Serra to found our state.

PART II

ST. JOSEPH AND BLESSED JOSEPH MARELLO, FOUNDER OF THE OBLATES OF ST. JOSEPH

Originally given at the Sixth International Symposium on Saint Joseph, held in Rome, September 12-19, 1993. The beatification ceremony took place on September 26, 1993. The presentation was originally published in *Cahiers de Joséphologie*, Vol. XLIII (1995), Montreal.

It is with great pleasure that I develop the theme "St. Joseph and Blessed Joseph Marello," on the occasion of the trip of Pope John Paul II to Asti to officially declare him *"Blessed* Joseph Marello." His beatification not only provides another inspiring model for the faithful; it not only honors the dioceses of Asti and Acqui and my congregation, the Oblates of St. Joseph; it also directly witnesses to the power for sanctification found in St. Joseph's example and intercession. Marello learned and attained holiness at the school of St. Joseph.

This Second Part will consist of three principal sections: first, a description of Marello's devotion to St. Joseph throughout his life; second, a study of the virtues that Marello's writings find in St. Joseph; and finally, the thesis that Marello's holiness consisted in imitating St. Joseph's virtues.

DEVOTION TO ST. JOSEPH THROUGHOUT BLESSED MARELLO'S LIFE

Personal Patronage given with his name "Joseph"

Marello's life began under St. Joseph's patronage from the day of his birth on December 26, 1844, when he was baptized "Joseph" the very same day. His paternal grandfather was also *Giuseppe* and his maternal grandmother *Giuseppa*. This name was to determine his life-long relationship with his "holy patron."[128]

Among his personal notes during his seminary years, we find reference to "my protector Joseph" along with his resolve to love only God, in his "saints, in Mary, in Joseph..."[129] As March 28, 1868 approaches, the date of his reception of the subdiaconate, he prefers to anticipate the obligation

---

[128] *"Nostro S. Patrono."* Letter 62, 3/17/1870. Letters are found in M. PASETTI, *Le Lettere del Venerabile Giuseppe Marello*, Asti Italy 1979.

[129] *"Voglio amare Voi solo fonte d'ogni Amore, ... nei vostri santi, in Maria, in Gius., ... mio protettore Giuseppe."* Reflections, 1866-67, Impressions on reading the life of Alacoque. All quotes from Marello not in letters are found in M. PASETTI, *Scritti e Insegnamenti del Venerabile Giuseppe Marello*, Asti Italy 1980. A Spanish translation of this is *Los Escritos y Las Enseñanzas del Bienaventurado José Marello*, Santa Cruz California 1993.

of reciting the Liturgy of the Hours so that he may begin on St. Joseph's Day, March 19.

In his letters to others named Joseph, Marello delighted in referring to them as his "namesakes." During his first year of priesthood he wrote his classmate Joseph Riccio:

> Beloved namesake: ... Now then, Friday is St. Joseph's day; ... anniversary of the first recitation of the Divine Office ... It's agreed then, that on Friday we will remember that both of us bear the name Joseph and both of us will implore the patronage of our great namesake"[130]

Exactly twenty years later, right after his ordination as Bishop and as he is preparing to enter his diocese, he recalls three other Josephs on the vigil of their common feast: Bishop Joseph Sciandra, his predecessor in the See of Acqui, "the ancient Joseph," while he himself is the "new Joseph;" Monsignor Joseph Pagella, who will be his Vicar General; and Bishop Joseph Ronco of Asti. He writes:

> The ancient Joseph who is already in heaven with his patron has yielded his title for these

---

[130]*"Omonimo amatissimo, ... Dunque Venerdì è S. Giuseppe: ...* Anniversario *della prima recitazione del divino ufficio, ... Venerdì ci ricorderemo nel S. Sacrificio che tutti e due abbiam nome Giuseppe e che tutti e due domandiamo il patrocinio del Nostro Grande Omonimo."* Letter 35, after 3/13/1869.

prayers to the new Joseph, and I will take advantage of this immediately... Oh how many things will I say to the glorious patriarch whose name I bear! And for the Vicar, my namesake? There will come to my aid in these prayers the angel Joseph of Asti concerned along with me to perform this task of charity.[131]

Over 120 of Marello's letters between 1869 and 1895 bear the initials J.M.J. in one way or another, at times in Latin, at times with the Italian letters "*W.G.M.G.*," meaning "Long live Jesus, Mary and Joseph."

Proclamation of Universal Patronage of St. Joseph

While Marello was still a newly ordained priest, his personal patron, St. Joseph, received universal recognition. Marello's first assignment was to be secretary to his Bishop. If this position involved sacrificing his eagerness for parish ministry, it also brought with it the blessing of being able to accompany Bishop Savio to the First Vatican Council. A

---

[131]"*L'antico Giuseppe che è già in cielo col suo Patrono ha ceduto il titolo suo per queste preghiere al nuovo Giuseppe e io me ne valgo fin d'ora ... oh quante cose dirò al glorioso Patriarca di cui porto il nome! E pel Vicario mio omonimo? Mi verrà in aiuto in queste preghiere il Giuseppe Angelo della Diocesi d'Asti con me interessato a compiere quest'ufficio di carità.*" Letter 151, 3/18/1889.

letter of his from Rome during this period shows his enthusiasm at the presentation of the petition made by 38 cardinals, 153 bishops and 43 superiors general:

> Two days before the feast of our holy patron, at a time when devotion to the head of the holy family is about to attain its highest development through Christianity's petitions to the Vatican Council fathers ... let us both pray in unison on the day of our great patriarch that, by beginning to exalt him in our hearts, we may be made worthy to see him exalted soon by all of Christianity under the title being prepared for him: "Patron of the Universal Church" ... Long live St. Joseph with his devotees.[132]

Although the council was interrupted, the December 8, 1870 Decree *Quemadmodum Deus* and that of July 7, 1871, *Inclitum Patriarcham*, not only brought joy to his heart, but also oriented the remainder of his priestly ministry in the ways of St. Joseph.

---

[132] *"All'antivigilia del nostro S. Patrono e in momenti in cui la devozione al Capo della Sacra Famiglia sta per toccare il suo più alto sviluppo mercé le petizioni fatte dalla Cristianità ai Padri del Vaticano Concilio ... Preghiamo tutti e due d'accordo nel giorno del nostro grande Patriarca, affinché cominciandolo ad esaltare noi nel nostro cuore ci rendiamo degni di vederlo esaltato prossimamente da tutta la Cristianità col titolo che gli si sta preparando di Patrono della Chiesa Universale... . Viva S. Giuseppe coi suoi devoti."* Letter 62.

Marello's response with the idea of a Company of St. Joseph

By 1872 the zealous young priest's experience in Rome found expression in his design for a lay "Company of St. Joseph to promote the interests of Jesus, after the example of St. Joseph." He suggested that it be founded at the Church named *Il Gesù* in Asti:

> Each member draws inspiration from his exemplar St. Joseph, who was the first on earth to look after the interests of Jesus; he guarded him in his infancy; he protected him in his boyhood; he acted as his father during the first thirty years of his life on earth.[133]

The established clergy in Asti were not yet open to such an idea, and rather than yield to disappointment at not being able to see such a plan realized, Marello had to trust all the more in divine providence.

After five years of spiritual maturing, however, he was to draft another outline for a "Company of St. Joseph." This time, though, he was not thinking simply of a lay society, but of men living the gospel

---

[133]*"Compagnia di S. Giuseppe promotrice degli interessi di Gesù.... Ognuno prende le proprie ispirazioni dal suo Modello S. Giuseppe che fu il primo sulla terra a curare gli interessi di Gesù esso che ce lo custodì infante e lo protesse fanciullo e gli fu in luogo di padre nei primi trent'anni della sua vita qui in terra."* Letter 76, 10/25/1872.

counsels in community as religious, but without
vows. By imitating St. Joseph's hidden life, the
members could become true disciples of Christ:

> Whoever ... desires to follow closely the
> Divine Master by the observance of the
> evangelical counsels, is welcome to the house
> of St. Joseph. Withdrawing therein with the
> resolve to remain hidden and silently active
> in imitation of the great model of a poor and
> obscure life, he will have an opportunity to
> become a true disciple of Jesus Christ.[134]

By St. Joseph's month the following year, said
congregation was founded. The first members were
simply Oblate Brothers, non-professed. The only
decoration in their room was an unframed paper
picture of St. Joseph, a witness to their imitation of
his poverty. Fr. Cortona, Marello's first successor
and biographer, writes that the "primary goal would
be to honor St. Joseph and to imitate his virtues,

---

[134]*"Compagnia di S. Giuseppe. A chi ... desideri di seguire dappresso il divin Maestro
coll'osservanza dei Consigli Evangelici, è aperta la Casa di S. Giuseppe, dove, ritirandosi col
proposito di permanervi, nascostamente e silenziosamente operoso, nell'imitazione di quel grande
Modello di vita povera ed oscura, avrà modo di farsi vero discepolo di Gesù Cristo."* Letter 95,
11/4/1877.

patterning themselves after the great patriarch's poor, humble, and hidden life."[135]

It was truly St. Joseph who guided and protected Marello's congregation at each step, much as he guided and protected Marello himself. It was after a novena to St. Joseph, in 1883, that Marello took the important step of accepting the petition to allow some Oblate brothers to begin studies for the priesthood. When Fr. Baratta, the first of these brothers, was ready for ordination, the brothers were praying to St. Joseph at the time that Bishop Ronco made the difficult decision to permit Oblates to become priests. It is because Marello had St. Joseph's trust in divine providence that he was able to allow the form of the congregation to adapt to the unfolding of circumstances.

When Marello had to leave the congregation behind to become Bishop of Acqui, he exhorted the brethren to a firm trust in St. Joseph, especially in economic difficulties. Although he would have to leave, St. Joseph would always remain with them, more trustworthy than Napoleon who used to tell

---

[135]"... avessero per fine principale di onorare S. Giuseppe, imitandone le virtù e cercando di uniformare la loro vita con quella povera, umile e nascosta del grande patriarca." G. B. CORTONA, Brevi Memorie della Vita di Mons. Giuseppe Marello, ch. III, Asti Italy 1920. An English translation is Brief Memories of the Life of Joseph Marello, Santa Cruz California 1993.

his soldiers: "Never fear; never fear; Napoleon is here."[136]

While Marello was Bishop in Acqui, providence began to indicate that the Oblates should move toward official status as a religious congregation. The first Rules of 1892 state that by the practice of the evangelical counsels, the confreres will imitate St. Joseph, a model of poverty, chastity and obedience for all religious to imitate, but particularly for the Oblates who bear his name, who consider themselves his sons and who dedicate themselves to imitating his particular virtues, which we will examine later, and to fostering devotion to him. He is their special patron:

> The congregation has for its patron St. Joseph. For this reason its members are called "Oblates of St. Joseph" and strive to honor and love him as a father by imitating his virtues and spreading his devotion.[137]

In the last years of Marello's life, the congregation underwent very difficult trials that threatened its very survival. The founder unfailingly exhorted

---

[136] *"Je suis Napoleon: (ne) tremblez pas, (ne) tremblez pas!"* P. A. GARBEROGLIO, in *Positio Super Virtutibus*, Rome 1974, 272.

[137] *"La Congregazione ha per Patrono S. Giuseppe, perciò i membri suoi sono chiamati OBLATI DI S. GIUSEPPE e si fanno studio speciale di onorarlo e di amarlo come padre, imitandone le virtù e propagandone la devozione."* Rules, ch. I.

the brethren to have confidence in St. Joseph's protection, a confidence he maintained to the end and a protection which was never lacking.

Other Initiatives at St. Clare's and in Acqui

Marello's devotion to St. Joseph was not limited only to the founding of the Oblates. It also permeated all his pastoral ministry.

At St. Clare's,[138] the first house owned by the Oblates, he established the Wednesday celebration of the Seven Sorrows and Joys of St. Joseph. He introduced the month of March devotions in which the Sorrows and Joys were recited daily and a reading on St. Joseph's virtues accompanied Benediction. Besides celebration of the feast of the Patronage of St. Joseph after Easter, he began the solemn celebration of March 19 along with the preparatory novena.

Multiple witnesses testify[139] that Marello did not merely promote prayer devotions to St. Joseph, but that his preaching above all emphasized taking him as a model and imitating his virtues and his total dedication to Jesus. Marello's devotion to St. Joseph

---

[138] cf. *Positio Super Introductione Causae*, Rome 1946; 92, 139, 214.
[139] e.g. *Positio S. Virt.*, 233.

was truly Christocentric, in the sense described by Vatican II.[140]

Marello had also initiated at St. Clare's a group of Daughters of St. Joseph and invested them with a medal of St. Joseph, but the Vincentian Sisters suppressed them after Marello's departure for Acqui in 1889.

From the time of his ordination as Bishop, Marello recommended the faithful of his new diocese to the patronage of St. Joseph, the Guardian of the Holy Family.[141] He encouraged the Sisters of Ovada to take the Family of Nazareth as the model for their communities.

Marello's first pontifical Mass at St. Clare's was on St. Joseph's day, March 19, 1889. On the eve of the feast, he wrote: "Tomorrow St. Joseph will receive many prayers for the Bishop and for the Vicar of the Diocese of Acqui."[142]

Once installed in his new Diocese, he issued a circular letter to his clergy on September 16, 1889, communicating Leo XIII's *Quamquam Pluries* on devotion to Mary and Joseph: "... the maternal protection of the Most Holy Virgin, the patronage

---

[140] cf. *Lumen Gentium*, no. 50.

[141] Letter 150, 3/16/1889.

[142] *"Domani S. Giuseppe riceverà molte preghiere pel Vescovo e pel Vicario della Diocesi d'Acqui."* Letter 151.

of her glorious husband St. Joseph assist you in every moment."[143] On March 11, 1891 he communicated to his clergy the apostolic letter *Quod Erat* establishing for Piedmont, Liguria, Sardegna and Lombardy that March 19 be a holy day of obligation. His September 24, 1892 circular letter for the fiftieth episcopal anniversary of Leo XIII, conveyed the papal brief *Neminem Fugit* for the establishment of the Universal Association of Families consecrated to the Holy Family of Nazareth, as an efficacious remedy for the decadence and materialism of the time.

The last months of Marello's life witnessed a controversy with the Little House of Divine Providence of Turin over possession of St. Clare's. Although this dispute threatened the very existence of the Oblates of St. Joseph, Marello remained always composed and kind, abandoning himself to divine providence after the example of his patron and constantly exhorting the brethren to trust in St. Joseph's powerful protection.

One example of the efficaciousness of this trust occurred on March 28, 1895, when he sent the Theresian Sisters of Ovada in his diocese to replace

---

[143]"… *la materna tutela della Santissima Vergine, Il Patrocinio del suo Inclito Sposo S. Giuseppe vi assistano in ogni istante della vita.*"

the Vincentian Sisters, who were withdrawn from St. Clare's during the crisis. The Theresians, now known as the Daughters of Our Lady of Mercy, had just been making a novena to St. Joseph to find a ministry, and they certainly found it at St. Clare's from where they developed.

The painful events of the controversy nevertheless seem to have taken their toll on Marello's health. When human criteria would indicate that his presence was most needed, he offered his life as a holocaust for the welfare of the congregation that was founded on divine providence and that would continue on the same foundation. His last written words to the congregation noted that in imitation of their patron, the Brothers of St. Joseph more than at any other time were experiencing joys mingled with sorrows. His closing sentence exhorted and still exhorts his Oblates to "be in good spirits under the fatherly mantle of St. Joseph, a place of safest refuge in trials and tribulations."[144]

Blessed Marello's life begins and ends under this mantle of St. Joseph, his life-long patron, protector and model.

---

[144] *"State tutti di buon animo sotto il paterno manto di S. Giuseppe, luogo di sicurissimo rifugio in tribulationibus et angustiis."* Letter 278, 3/4/1895.

THE VIRTUES OF ST. JOSEPH IN MARELLO'S WRITINGS AND TEACHINGS

After this brief overview of the place of devotion to St. Joseph in Marello's life, it should be helpful to analyze the virtues he saw in St. Joseph and presented to others for imitation, especially in his counsels and spiritual writings. Though these will be categorized into sections here, it must be realized that Marello left us no written treatise on these virtues and that in fact they are all very interconnected, finding their unity in the person of St. Joseph, the man most intimately connected with the mystery of the incarnation of the Son of God.

Conformity to God's will, Peace of Soul, Trust in Divine Providence

It may seem like the three phrases in the title of this section should be dealt with individually since they refer to quite distinct traits. The picture we get from Marello's spirituality, however, is that they are really inseparable aspects of a basic attitude of faith that characterized St. Joseph. His constant conformity to God's will expressed an unfailing trust in God's providence and resulted in a peace of soul that did not depend on the variable circumstances of life's ups and downs. Marello's counsel to Miss Bice Graglia summarizes this:

[St. Joseph remained] ever calm, peaceful and tranquil, observing in everything a perfect conformity to God's wishes. St. Joseph desired nothing, wanted nothing that was not for the greater glory of God. He was thus always imperturbable, even in adversities. Let us model ourselves after this sublime example and let us learn to remain peaceful and tranquil in all of life's circumstances.[145]

The following quotes from Marello beautifully emphasize these same ideas without need of commentary:

Let the foundation of the Company of St. Joseph rest on ground that is firm and stable ... let everything proceed according to the dictates of faith, with a boundless trust in the help of Heaven and an unfailing grati-

---

[145] "... mantenendosi sempre calmo, sempre sereno e tranquillo, osservando in tutto una perfetta conformità ai voleri di Dio. S. Giuseppe non desiderava nulla, non voleva nulla che non fosse del maggior piacere di Dio. Quindi era sempre imperturbabile, anche nelle avversità. Specchiamoci in questo sublime modello ed impariamo a mantenerci calmi e tranquilli in tutte le circostanze della vita." 3/22/1889.

tude to God alone, whether in abundance or privation.[146]

We should be at peace even with respect to our spiritual life, so that although we make constant effort to progress, we do not worry at all about knowing whether we are going forward or backward in perfection. We should ask St. Joseph for peace and equanimity of soul. He was always even-tempered with himself, whether he was commanding Jesus, Wisdom of the Father, or whether he was exercising his trade, busy with humble manual labor. If St. Joseph did not grant favors, he would no longer be St. Joseph.[147]

In this life joy and pain are forever alternating ... And yet, was not the life of St. Joseph also a succession of consolations and fears? Let St. Clare's, then, be like the house of St. Joseph. In the midst of doubts and

---

[146] "... si gettino le basi della Compagnia di S. Giuseppe sopra un terreno stabile e fermo ... tutto proceda per principi di fede con una illimitata confidenza negli aiuti del cielo e un sentimento indefettibile di riconoscenza al Signore ed a Lui solo tanto nell'abbondanza come nel difetto..." Letter 76.

[147] "Bisogna star tranquilli anche riguardo alla nostra vita spirituale, in modo che pur sforzandoci continuamente di progredire, non ci preoccupiamo affatto di sapere se andiamo avanti o indietro nella perfezione. Bisogna chiedere a S. Giuseppe la tranquillità e l'eguaglianza di spirito. Egli era uguale a se stesso, sia quando comandava a Gesù, Sapienza del Padre, sia quando esercitava il suo mestiere, occupandosi dei lavori più umili e grossolani. Se S. Giuseppe non facesse grazie non sarebbe più S. Giuseppe." Counsel to Sr. A. Fasolis, 5/20/1884.

anxieties, let all hearts rest trustful and secure. Let everyone repeat with St. Paul: "I am content with my distress for Christ's sake."[148]

So we shall say to our great patriarch: We belong entirely to you, and may you be all ours. Show us the way. Support us at every step. Guide us where Divine Providence wants us to go. No matter how long or short our journey, no matter how smooth or rough, whether by human sight we glimpse our goal or not, whether our pace is fast or slow, with you we are sure of always going along the right path.[149]

Interior Life and Union with Jesus

Pope John Paul II's Apostolic Exhortation on St. Joseph has a chapter entitled "The Primacy of the

---

[148]"*In questo mondo sempre si avvicendano il gaudio e la pena … E la vita di S. Giuseppe non fu anch'essa un'alternativa di consolazioni e di timori? Dunque in S. Chiara, come nella Casa di S. Giuseppe, in mezzo ai dubbi e all'ansietà siano gli animi sempre fiduciosi e sicuri e si ripeta da tutti con S. Paolo: Placeo mihi in angustiis pro Christo.*" Letter 198, 10/24/1890, with reference to 2 Cor. 12:10.

[149]"*Diremo dunque al nostro Grande Patriarca: Eccoci tutti per Te e Tu sii tutto per noi. Tu ci segna la via, ci sorreggi in ogni passo, ci conduci dove la Divina Provvidenza vuole che arriviamo, sia lungo o breve il cammino, piano o malagevole, si vegga o non si vegga per vista umana la meta. O in fretta o adagio noi con Te siam sicuri di andar sempre bene.*" Letter 208, 3/8/1891.

Interior Life."[150] From that chapter we understand that the trusting abandonment to God's will that we considered in the previous section can only result from St. Joseph's deep interior life. This official proclamation authoritatively confirms Marello's teaching of over a century ago that St. Joseph is a model of contemplation and union with Jesus: "Let us commend ourselves to St. Joseph, master and guide of the spiritual life, sublime model of the interior and hidden life."[151]

From St. Joseph's example we learn how to receive Christ into our lives spiritually and sacramentally as he did physically:

> When we receive Holy Communion, let us consider that Jesus comes to us as a little baby, and then let us pray that St. Joseph help us welcome Him, as when he held Him in his arms.[152]

In fact, St. Joseph is not only a model for us, but actually a teacher and guide. "St. Joseph, protector

---

[150] *Redemptoris Custos*, ch. 5, 8/15/1989.

[151] "*Raccomandiamoci al glorioso S. Giuseppe, guida e maestro della vita spirituale, sublime modello di vita interiore e nascosta.*" Counsel to Miss Bice Graglia, 3/15/1889.

[152] "*Quando si va alla Santa Comunione pensiamo che Gesù viene a noi come un piccolo Bambinello; e allora preghiamo S. Giuseppe che ci aiuti ad accoglierlo, come quando Egli lo teneva tra le Sue braccia.*" Counsel to Fasolis, undated.

of the interior life, be my teacher."[153] "Let us ask St. Joseph to act as our spiritual director."[154]

The "man closest to Jesus"[155] is able to also bring us close to Him: "Let us ask St. Joseph for familiarity and intimate union with Jesus."[156]

Common Virtues in Everyday Life, Humility, Hidden Life

Again the various terms in this heading are simply different names for a single reality. What is probably most specifically characteristic of Marello's Josephite spirituality is his uncompromised conviction of the importance of humility and the hidden life, of doing our ordinary and everyday tasks with great love and dedication:

> Look at Jesus, Mary and Joseph, the three greatest persons to live on this earth. What did they do at Nazareth? Nothing that appeared great or extraordinary. They simply performed the humble, ordinary tasks of a

---

[153] *"S. Giuseppe, protettore della vita interiore, fatemi da Maestro."* Counsel to Fasolis, 3/15/1889.

[154] *"A S. Giuseppe chiediamo che ci faccia da direttore spirituale."* Counsel to Fasolis, 3/8/1888.

[155] Title from monumental work of F. L. FILAS, *Joseph the Man Closest to Jesus*, Boston 1962.

[156] *"A S. Giuseppe chiediamo la familiarità e l'unione intima con Gesù."* Counsel to Fasolis 3/1/1888.

poor working family. Yet all their actions were motivated by a spirit of prayerful union with God and therefore took on tremendous glory and worth in the sight of heaven. Hence, it is not a question of doing great and extraordinary things, but of doing God's will in everything. Whether the tasks entrusted to us be great or small, we only need to fulfill God's will in obedience and they will bring us great merit.[157]

This insight helps us appreciate Jesus' parable of the mustard seed (Mt. 13:31-35) which precedes the question of his countryfolk (Mt. 13:54b-55): "Where did he get this wisdom and these miracles? Isn't this the carpenter's son?" Here is an excerpt from Marello's 1886 homily on the parable:

The mustard seed is considered the smallest of all seeds that are sown in the garden and yet it grows to form a large bush. It therefore represents well the small virtues which can

---

[157] *"Guardate Gesù, Maria e Giuseppe, i tre più grandi personaggi che siano vissuti su questa terra. Che cosa facevano essi in Nazaret? Nulla di grande e di straordinario in apparenza; non attendevano che ad occupazioni umili ed ordinarie, proprie di una povera famiglia operaia. Ma essendo essi animati dallo spirito di orazione e di unione con Dio tutte le loro azioni assumevano un valore ed uno splendore immenso agli occhi del cielo. Non si tratta dunque di fare azioni grandi e straordinarie, ma di fare in ogni cosa la volontà di Dio. Siano piccoli o grandi gli uffici che ci vengono affidati; basta che li facciamo per ubbidienza alla volontà di Dio e acquisteremo in essi grandi meriti."* Retreat preached at Milliavacca Institute, beginning 10/8/1881.

produce great sanctity. In fact the great
saints did not attain sanctity so much by the
practice of the extraordinary virtues, for
which there are few opportunities, as by
repeated and constant acts of the small
virtues. Thus St. Joseph did not do extraordinary things, but rather by the constant practice of the ordinary and common virtues he
attained that sanctity which elevates him
above all the other saints.[158]

Sanctity, therefore, is not limited to martyrs and
others who do heroic deeds:

Courage then, and may St. Lawrence help
us… But could St. Lawrence take us far from
St. Joseph? Here too I trust the ability of the
homilist to find the analogies between the
Patriarch and the Levite. It is not always the
fire which makes the grate hot.[159]

---

[158] *"Il granello di senape viene considerato come il seme più piccolo di quanti se ne seminano nell'orto e tuttavia si sviluppa tanto da formare un bell' alberello; perciò esso raffigura bene le piccole virtù, le quali possono produrre una gran santità. Infatti i grandi santi raggiunsero la loro santità non tanto per la pratica delle virtù straordinarie, delle quali sono molto rare le occasioni, ma con gli atti ripetuti e incessanti delle piccole virtù. Così S. Giuseppe non fece cose straordinarie; ma colla pratica costante delle virtù ordinarie e comuni raggiunse quella santità che lo eleva al di sopra di tutti gli altri santi."* Milliavacca preaching, 2/14/1886.

[159] *"Coraggio dunque e S. Lorenzo ci aiuti…. Ma S. Lorenzo ci porterà lungi da S. Giuseppe? Anche qui all'abilità del panegirista il trovare le analogie tra il Patriarca e il Levita. Non è sempre il fuoco che fa rovente la graticola."* Letter 157, 8/8/1889.

In other words, the penances of everyday life may have the merits of martyrdom, if done with St. Joseph's spirit of dedication. Unlike many religious people in his time, Marello did not encourage a great deal of mortification, but rather emphasized a holy attitude towards daily difficulties, for that is what characterized Mary and Joseph:

> It is not necessary to resort to extraordinary penances. It is sufficient to practice the penance of enduring each day everything that God disposes, ... not only on occasion, but constantly. This penance may seem easy and ordinary, but it is more demanding and of greater worth than extraordinary penance.... Mary Most Holy and St. Joseph practiced this penance. They were not known or admired by the world, but they were most well known to God. Let us imitate Mary Most Holy and St. Joseph in their ordinary penance. Let them be our models.[160]

---

160 *"Non è necessario ricorrere a penitenze straordinarie, basta praticare la penitenza ordinaria, che consiste nel soffrire giornalmente tutto quello Dio dispone, ... e questo non qualche volta soltanto, ma costantemente; questa può parere una penitenza facile ed ordinaria, ma costa di più ed è di maggior merito che la penitenza straordinaria.... Maria SS. e S. Giuseppe praticarono questa penitenza: essi non erano conosciuti ed ammirati dal mondo, ma da Dio erano conosciutissimi. Imitiamo Maria SS. e S. Giuseppe nella loro penitenza ordinaria: siano essi i nostri esemplari."* Milliavacca preaching, 12/19/1886.

Three additional quotes show that Marello considered St. Joseph a universal model in this regard, and in a particular way a model for families and for working brothers, since he sanctified himself in the same daily circumstances in which they find themselves:

> Let us invoke and imitate Mary Most Holy and St. Joseph, whose humility was truly heroic, and let us take them as models and intercessors to obtain this precious virtue.[161]

> [St. Joseph] also found himself in the same situations that we do in our family life. Let us imitate him in the practice of those common and hidden virtues, which so please God and so help the soul progress in sanctity.[162]

The student brothers must have a high regard for the working brothers, since these by their humble labor imitate more closely the humble worker of Nazareth, St. Joseph,

---

[161] *"Preghiamo ed imitiamo Maria SS. e S. Giuseppe, la cui umiltà fu veramente eroica, e prendiamoli come modelli ed intercessori nell'acquisto di questa preziosa virtù."* Milliavacca Preaching, 12/3/1886.

[162] *"[S. Giuseppe] pure si trovò nelle medesime nostre circostanze nella sua vita familiare: imitiamolo nella pratica di quelle virtù comuni e nascoste, che tanto piacciono a Dio e tanto aiutano l'anima a progredire e santificarsi."* Counsel to Graglia, 3/15/1889.

the patron and exemplar of the congregation.[163]

Exemplar of the Religious Life of Poverty, Chastity and Obedience

While St. Joseph's common virtues are a model
for everyone, each in his particular state of life,
Marello sees him also as the first model of religious
life in particular, a paragon of poverty, chastity and
obedience:

> [By the practice of the evangelical coun-
> sels, the Oblate] will imitate St. Joseph, the
> first exemplar of the religious life, who had
> continually under his gaze the Divine Exem-
> plar, sent to the world by the Eternal Father
> in His mercy to teach the way to Heaven.[164]

The "first exemplar of religious life," is exemplar of
each of the evangelical counsels. Poverty is related
to the humble and hidden life discussed above "in
imitation of that great model of a poor and obscure

---

[163] "*I Fratelli studenti devono avere una grande stima per quelli che sono addetti ai lavori,
come quelli che lavorando nella umiltà imitano più da vicino l'umile fabbro di Nazaret, S.
Giuseppe, patrono e modello della Congregazione.*" Rules, ch. 2.

[164] "*... con la pratica dei Consigli evangelici; per imitare così S. Giuseppe che fu il primo
modello della vita religiosa, avendo avuto egli continuamente sotto gli occhi quell'Esemplare
Divino, che l'Eterno Padre per sua misericordia volle mandare al mondo perché insegnasse la via
del Cielo.*" Rules, ch.1.

life."[165] The traditional symbol of St. Joseph, the lily, signifies his outstanding chastity: "The Sons of St. Joseph must strive to love chastity so as to imitate their patron St. Joseph, who was a spotless lily of chastity."[166] St. Joseph desires obedience to be the "safeguard"[167] of unity and of a religious society:

> Ah, obedience! ... How many graces does not obedience draw down from Heaven to keep us from taking a false step and to guide us directly to our goal! Let us mourn the fact that not a few brothers allowed the tender shoots of this virtue to wither, while St. Joseph wanted it deeply rooted in their hearts.... St. Joseph will intercede for us.[168]

While St. Joseph is a model for all religious, he is especially so for Marello's Oblates: "The Congregation of St. Joseph ... is named after this saint because it chose him as the pattern of its life and

---

[165] Letter 95.

[166] "*I Figli di S. Giuseppe debbono procurare di essere amanti della castità, per imitare così il loro patrono S. Giuseppe che fu giglio illibatissimo di castità.*" Rules, ch. 5.

[167] "*La carità è il vincolo della unità e l'ubbidienza ne è la salvaguardia.*" Letter 76.

[168] "*Ah l'ubbidienza ... quante grazie ci attira dal cielo per non mettere il piede in fallo e per andar dritti alla meta! Addoloriamoci che non pochi Fratelli abbiano lasciato inaridire i germogli di questa virtù che S. Giuseppe voleva ben radicar nei loro cuori; ... S. Giuseppe intercederà per noi.*" Letter 234, 4/4/1892.

appointed him as its special patron."[169] Imitation of St. Joseph leads to "a tender devotion to the Sacred Heart of Jesus ... especially in His Sacrament of Love."[170] Of course, it is not possible to "imitate St. Joseph without loving and honoring his beloved spouse Mary."[171]

Exemplar of Ministry

Since St. Joseph is thought to have died before Jesus began His public ministry, we do not usually associate him with apostolate, as we do with families, workers, contemplatives, religious. Pope John Paul II, however, declares that his noble example "transcends all individual states of life and serves as a model for the entire Christian community."[172] He is an "exceptional teacher in the service of Christ's saving mission" also for "those called to the apostolate."[173] In the nineteenth century, Marello saw St.

---

[169] *"La Congregazione di S. Giuseppe ha per iscopo la santificazione dei suoi componenti. Si chiama col nome di tal Santo, sì perché lo scelse qual modello del suo vivere, sì perché lo prese qual patrono speciale."* Rules, ch. 1.

[170] *"... una tenera devozione al S Cuore di Gesù ... specialmente nel suo Sacramento d'Amore."* Rules, ch. 1.

[171] *"Non si potrebbe poi imitare S. Giuseppe, senza onorare ed amare la sua diletta Sposa Maria."* Rules, ch. 1.

[172] *Redemptoris Custos*, 30.

[173] *Redemptoris Custos*, 32.

Joseph as a model first for his own priestly ministry and later for that of the Congregation he founded.

A few days before his ordination to the subdeaconate, he wrote:

> Oh glorious patriarch St. Joseph ... be our exemplar in our ministry, which like your own is a ministry of intimate relationship with the Divine Word. May you teach us, may you assist us, may you render us worthy members of the Holy Family.[174]

In his very first "Design for a Company of St. Joseph," we find: "St. Joseph, welcome us as your companions in the ministries which you merited to perform on earth."[175] We tend today to understand ministry and apostolate as a series of tasks that St. Joseph never had the opportunity to perform. Marello saw more deeply, however, that the essence of ministry is rooted in a relationship with Jesus that results in dedicated service to the "interests of Jesus."[176] Since, after Mary, no one did this better than Joseph, he is quite fittingly a model for apostles as well as contemplatives.

---

[174] *"O glorioso patriarca S. Giuseppe ... sii il nostro esemplare nel nostro ministero che, come il tuo, è ministero di relazione intima col Divin Verbo; Tu ci ammaestra ci assisti ci rendi degni membri della Sacra Famiglia."* Letter 35.

[175] *"Sancte Joseph ... accipe nos comites tuos in ministeriis quae in terris persolvere meruisti."* Letter 76.

[176] *"... gli interessi di Gesù."* Letter 76.

A particular area in which Marello applied this insight was in the ministry to youth, so emphasized in his Congregation of Oblates. The Lenten catechism classes taught to workers at St. Agnes Church in 1884 were taught beneath a picture of St. Joseph teaching Jesus to read. In the ministry of teaching religion, the Oblates are to imitate the charity and dedication with which St. Joseph performed his fatherly duty of teaching the Son of God Incarnate.

Director, Guardian, Guide, Protector of the Oblates of St. Joseph

All the sub-sections of this second section have described virtues and characteristics of St. Joseph that we may somehow imitate. This is in accord with the Church's desire that we take the saints as models, as well as intercessors. Marello clearly emphasized this imitation of St. Joseph, as we have seen. In section one we also saw what great trust Marello placed in St. Joseph's patronage in his own life and also for the congregation he founded. As a conclusion to section two, the following quotes exemplify Marello's beautiful and heart-felt descriptions of St. Joseph's all-encompassing role in the congregation:

"St. Joseph is our lawyer in Heaven, ... our defender, and even more our father, and we are his clients whom he defends, his children...."[177]

"St. Joseph is always the Choir Director who intones the songs, although he sometimes allows a few false notes. Nevertheless, in this his dear month he wishes all the notes to flow harmoniously."[178]

"The illness of Bro. Paul would make me very sad indeed, if I did not realize that St. Joseph is the infirmarian...."[179]

"May St. Joseph teach us how to take care of our aspirants; or rather, may he himself be their guardians."[180]

"Let us go together to Joseph and pray for one another."[181]

"... to the sons of this great common father ... greetings [also] to the ninety students who form the

---

[177] "S. Giuseppe è il nostro avvocato in cielo, ... il nostro patrocinante anzi il nostro Padre e noi siamo i suoi clienti, i suoi patrocinati, i suoi figli." Milliavacca preaching, 4/22/1888.

[178] "S. Giuseppe è sempre il Maestro di Cappella che dà le intonazioni, ma che qualche volta permette le piccole stonature. In questo suo caro mese però vuole che tutte le note fluiscano giuste e melodiose...." Letter 206, 2/23/1891.

[179] "L'infermità di Fr. Paolo mi rattristerebbe assai se non pensassi che è S. Giuseppe l'infermiere...." Letter 167, 11/8/1889.

[180] "S. Giuseppe c'insegni il modo di custodirli [i Fratelli], o meglio ne sia Lui il Custode." Letter 170, 11/23/1889.

[181] "Eamus simul ad Joseph et oremus pro invicem." Letter 205, 2/21/1891.

minor family of the great Patriarch and also have a right to his fatherly caresses."[182]

"I rejoice at the news that our dear sick are improving somewhat. May St. Joseph complete his task."[183]

When Fr. Cortona was to preach at St. Secundus: "As previously in so many other circumstances, so also in these, St. Joseph will not deny his effective influence to obtain from God the grace implored by so many hearts."[184]

BLESSED MARELLO'S HOLINESS CONSISTED OF IMITATING SAINT JOSEPH

Joseph Marello had a life-long devotion to his patron St. Joseph and he presented him to others as a model whose virtues they should imitate. We may nevertheless ask: Why is he "Blessed"? His life is

---

[182] *"... ai Figli di questo gran Padre comune ... auguri [anche ai] novanta alunni che formano la famiglia minore del grande Patriarca ed hanno pur diritto alle sue carezze paterne."* Letter 233, 3/19/1892.

[183] *"Godo della notizia che i cari infermi vadano alquanto migliorando. Oh S. Giuseppe voglia compiere l'opera sua!"* Letter 236, 4/16/1892.

[184] *"S. Giuseppe come già in altre così nelle presenti circostanze non rifiuterà il suo valido appoggio per ottenere da Dio la grazia da tanti cuori implorata."* Letter 245, 1/4/1893.

not outstanding for miraculous occurrences, extraordinary achievements or worldly renown.[185] Even the congregation he founded is hardly famous: in the words of Fr. Cortona, it "ranks near last in God's house."[186] What then is special about Joseph Marello?

He Did the Common, Ordinary, Little Things out of Love for God

The opening paragraphs of the 1978 Vatican Decree on the heroism of Marello's virtues are an authoritative declaration of why the Church considered him worthy to be called "Venerable" and now "Blessed":

> "St. Joseph is the model of the humble, whom Christianity raises to great destinies; St. Joseph is the proof that to be good and authentic followers of Christ, great things are not necessary, but what are sufficient and necessary are the common virtues, human and simple, but true and authentic" (Paul VI, Allocution of 3/19/1969). To have per-

---

[185] Cf. E. DEMARCHI, "Lo straordinario e la santità in Monsignor Marello," *Certosini e apostoli*, Rome July-October 1965; *Holiness in the Ordinary*, Santa Cruz California 1993.

[186] "*Questa Congregazione sorta per l'ultima nella Casa di Dio....*" CORTONA, Preface. *Brief Memories*, 2.

ceived this truth, to have made it a principle of life for himself and for others, to have personally experienced it was the charism and commitment of Joseph Marello, founder of the Oblates of St. Joseph and Bishop of Acqui.[187]

Joseph Marello is "Blessed," not because of anything extraordinary to human appearance, but because of his authentic following of Christ in the ordinary and common events of each day. He is Blessed because he realized that this was the essence of St. Joseph's sanctity and he dedicated his life to imitating this excellent model. Marello is Blessed because the St. Joseph virtues that he presented to others, he first of all lived himself.

Like St. Joseph, Marello never wished or desired anything that was not for the greater glory of God. Rather than worry about human respect,[188] he concentrated on pleasing God. He was convinced that "it is precisely perfection in the little things

---

[187] *"'San Giuseppe è il modello degli umili, che il Cristianesimo solleva a grandi destini; San Giuseppe è la prova che per esser buoni e autentici seguaci di Cristo non occorrono grandi cose, ma bastano ed occorrono virtù comuni, umane, semplici, ma vere ed autentiche' (Paolo VI, Allocuzione, 19 marzo 1969). Avere percepito questa verità, averne fatto un principio di vita per sé e per gli altri, averla personalmente esperimentata è stato il carisma e l'impegno di Giuseppe Marello, fondatore degli Oblati di S. Giuseppe e Vescovo di Acqui."* Decree of Sacred Congregation for the Causes of the Saints, 6/12/1978. See p. 122.

[188] Cf. Marello's Fifth Pastoral Letter, "On Human Respect," 1/25/1893.

that can make us saints"[189] and so he was happy to do the common tasks that often go un-noticed, with a great love for Christ. His constant, repeated, small acts of kindness caused him to be known as "the good Bishop" and "another Francis de Sales." He lived his life serving the interests of Jesus in union with Mary and Joseph, as if he were in the house of Nazareth.

He Lived in Prayerful Union with God, Always Available to do His Will

As St. Joseph lived in daily communion with the Christ-child in the Holy Family, so Marello sought to live that same communion in his life of prayer. Soon after his ordination, in the midst of priestly zeal and early fervor, he had the insight to write: "Let us pray. In these days prayer has become our greatest, most powerful apostolate."[190] A few short years later he was twice inclined to become a contemplative Trappist monk.[191] Like St. Joseph, however, his vocation to prayer was not to be expressed in solitude alone but in active availability

---

[189] *"... è appunto la perfezione nelle piccole cose che può farci santi."* Counsel to Graglia 12/6/1888.

[190] *"Preghiamo. A questi giorni la preghiera è diventata il più grande, il più potente Apostolato."* Letter 22, 1/1/1869.

[191] CORTONA, "St. Joseph Living in the Congregation - Draft of a Rule," *Certosini*, Rome Nov. 1967; appendix of *Brief Memories*, Santa Cruz 1993, 167-168.

to God's will, whatever that might be. When his spiritual director, Bishop Savio, dissuaded him from being a Trappist, he obeyed without being able to see what God might want from him. He simply persevered in prayer, invoking the intercession of Mary and Joseph. God's plan was for him to found the congregation of Oblates to follow his spirituality of imitating St. Joseph's interior life and conformity to God's will. To the first Oblates:

> he communicated his own spirit and what he had learned about St. Joseph from long years of meditating on the works of St. Francis de Sales, whom he read with love and devotion. Above all he taught them of the interior life of St. Joseph.[192]

When he was asked to be Bishop of Acqui against his personal inclinations at a time when he seemed so needed in Asti, he at first hesitated out of humility, but then accepted as soon as he realized it was God's will. As he zealously ministered to the people in every region of his diocese, all noted that when he celebrated liturgy, he was deeply absorbed in prayer. In his last days on earth, he was able to pray at the shrine of Our Lady of Mercy in Savona where he had received his vocation as a child.

---

[192] CORTONA, *Brief Memories*, ch. 3.

He Lived a Humble and Hidden Life Like St. Joseph

Paradoxically, where Marello's holiness stands out most is in its hiddenness, after the example of St. Joseph, "the model of the humble." The greatest saint after Mary[193]

> lived for many years unknown in Egypt and then hidden in Nazareth ... and even after death he remained unknown, while God determined that only after fifteen centuries would he be given solemn honor.[194]

As Marello shared these reflections with the first Oblates, he would conclude: "So let us too be hidden from men, but under the eyes of God; unknown to men, yet dear and beloved to God."[195] Joseph Marello lived by this principle.

In spite of the many important positions Marello held in Asti and all the ministry he performed, Iole Graglia testified that he was little known in

---

[193] Cf. *Redemptoris Custos*, 20.

[194] "*S. Giuseppe vive molti anni sconosciuto in Egitto e poi nascosto in Nazaret.... anzi persino dopo la morte rimane sconosciuto, mentre Iddio dispose che appena dopo 15 secoli gli si rendesse un culto solenne.*" In CORTONA, *Brief Memories*, ch. 3.

[195] "*Siamo dunque anche noi nascosti agli uomini, ma sotto gli occhi di Dio; sconosciuti dagli uomini, ma cari e diletti a Dio.*" Idem.

Asti, "because he lived hidden."[196] In fact for a long
time people, including the new bishop, Ronco, did
not even know that he was the founder of the
congregation of brothers. Fr. Garberoglio testifies
that "Marello was very happy to be able to remain
hidden this way,"[197] letting Canon Cerruti appear to
be the founder. He called the brothers "Oblates"
because "by this humble name he wished to veil the
condition of true religious having vows like all other
religious."[198] When Bishop Ronco was asked for an
official report on Marello, he concludes his long list
of praises by saying:

> His life is an untiring practice of holy virtues,
> of zeal for the glory of God and the salvation
> of souls, and of charitable works for the
> poor. And all this treasure is hidden under
> the veil of the purest humility: "The one who
> humbles himself will be exalted." Meekness
> of soul shines through him as his faithful
> companion in his every action and as a noble
> insignia of even nobler victories.[199]

---

[196] "*Qui in Asti, Mons. Marello era poco conosciuto perché viveva nascostamente.*" *Positio Super Intro.*, 239.

[197] "*... il Marello era ben lieto di potersi così nascondere.*" *Positio Super Intro.*, 167.

[198] CORTONA, "Draft of a Rule," *Brief Memories*, Ap. 2, 170.

[199] "*La sua vita è un indefesso esercizio di sante virtù, di zelo per la gloria di Dio e per la salute delle anime, di opere misericordiose verso i poverelli. E tutto questo tesoro è nascosto sotto l'involucro della più schietta umiltà: Qui se humiliat exaltabitur. La mitezza d'animo in lui*

He Worked Hard with Great Dedication

A brief mention should also be made of the quality of *laboriosità*, dedication to hard work, that Marello saw in St. Joseph, the carpenter of Nazareth. For Marello work was simply an expression of the interior life and faithfulness to the little ordinary things, "an expression of love," as Pope John Paul II calls it in the title of chapter four of *Redemptoris Custos*. Marello's first Rules for the Oblates therefore exhort the confreres to "attend with the greatest zeal to the task assigned,"[200] interweaving prayer and work as "Carthusians and apostles"[201] after the example of St. Joseph, whose life "was spent in work ... [and] prayer."[202] Study, manual work, spiritual ministry all share the common denominator of being expressions of love for God and conformity to His will.

Marello had a special interest in working with youth because of the difficulties he himself had experienced as a youth, because of their situation of great spiritual need in his time, and because this

---

traspare fedele compagna in ogni atto, ed è nobile insegna di più nobili vittorie." Letter of Bishop Ronco to Msgr. Pagella, 11/24/1888, *Le Lettere*, 424.

[200]"*Ciascuno poi deve attendere con grande alacrità all'ufficio che gli viene assegnato...*" Rules, ch. 6.

[201]CORTONA, *Brief Memories*, ch. 3.

[202]"*La vita di S. Giuseppe fu consumata nel lavoro e ... nell'orazione.*" Rules, ch. 6.

ministry was so easily identified with St. Joseph's ministry of raising the Christ-child. He never excluded, however, any other ministry which providence might ask of him,[203] since like St. Joseph he wished to be God's instrument. Bishop Ronco's letter, quoted earlier, thus reports a long list of all the apostolates Marello performed, noting that he fulfilled all the tasks entrusted to him with dignified calm and firmness:

> He is capable of a phenomenal amount of activity, but without ever seeming overworked and without losing a minute of time, he always works with great peace and steady constancy.[204]

His Trust in Divine Providence, Equanimity and Peace of Soul

Marello's hard work as an expression of love was always accompanied by a deep trust in God's providence. As a newly ordained priest he took the attitude: "Let us plant; let us irrigate; but most of all let us keep our eyes constantly turned toward

---

[203] The Oblates were to be open to whatever ministry "Divine Providence shall point out from day to day — *quelle cose che di giorno in giorno la divina Provvidenza additerà di fare.*" Rules, ch. 1.

[204] "*Egli è dotato di una attività singolare, la quale senza mostrarsi affannosa o perdere un minuto di tempo, opera con molta tranquillità e pari costanza.*" Ronco to Pagella, 11/28/1888, *Le Lettere*, 422.

the divine Sun from which descends the kind warmth that causes supernatural growth."[205] One of the most recurrent themes throughout his life is divine providence. He imitated St. Joseph's spontaneous abandonment to the will of God in every circumstance, as well as the quiet equanimity that resulted from this abandonment. He lived his counsel: "Like Mary and Joseph in the little house of Nazareth, let us be resigned to God's will in whatever He disposes."[206] He served the Lord with joy[207] and held that Joseph as well as Mary merited the prayer-title "Cause of our Joy."[208]

Many witnesses testify to Marello's self-possession and unalterable patience. Letters and incidents from his seminary years show that such equanimity was not a natural personality trait, but rather something he consciously learned at the school of St. Joseph, as he counseled others: "Let us mirror this sublime model [St. Joseph] and let us learn to remain calm and peaceful in all of life's circum-

---

[205] *"… piantiamo irrighiamo ma soprattutto teniamo costantemente rivolta la pupilla al grande Astro divino da cui discende il calore benefico della soprannaturale fecondazione."* Letter 29, around 2/20/1869.

[206] *"Come Maria e S. Giuseppe nella casetta di Nazaret stiamo rassegnati al volere di Dio in tutto ciò che Egli dispone."* Counsel to Fasolis, undated.

[207] He was fond of quoting Psalm 100:2 of the Vulgate: *"Servite Domino in laetitia."*

[208] *"Causa nostrae laetitiae."* Counsel to Graglia, 4/16/1888.

stances."[209] Marello became a living model of what he taught the first Oblates about St. Joseph. Fr. Cortona writes:

> Indeed, he had acquired such equanimity of spirit that in his seventeen years with us he never seemed too depressed by setbacks, nor too overjoyed by prosperity, but always his same pleasant self.[210]

The episode of his maintaining a trustful calm during an earthquake that occurred as he was celebrating Mass[211] is symbolic of his approach to all of life's surprises.

Marello's congregation went through many difficulties for its foundation, for its opening to the priesthood, for its economic survival, and for the crisis with the Little House of Divine Providence which claimed ownership of its home and actually sought to absorb it. His heroic holiness is seen in the fact that he never lost his calm composure, but constantly exhorted the confreres to trust in God's providence and St. Joseph's unfailing intercession:

---

[209] *"Specchiamoci in questo sublime modello ed impariamo a mantenerci calmi e tranquilli in tutte le circostanze della vita."* Counsel to Graglia, 3/22/1889.

[210] *"Difatti egli aveva acquistato tale uguaglianza di spirito, che nei 17 anni vissuti in nostra compagnia non si vide mai né troppo abbattuto nelle contrarietà, né troppo allegro nelle prosperità, ma sempre uguale a se stesso, affabile."* Brief Memories, ch. 3.

[211] M. Martino, in *Positio Super Virt.*, 296-297.

"The Lord will provide through Holy Joseph's intercession."[212]

He Gave his Life for the Work of Jesus

St. Joseph fulfilled his earthly task of acting as father to the Son of God. When Christ was ready to begin his public mission, however, St. Joseph simply faded from the scene, as if to allow him to teach about his heavenly Father unimpeded by any confusing presence of an earthly father. He is fittingly known as the patron of a happy death.

Marello's entire life was spent in prayerfully active work for the interests of Jesus, "the service of God in imitation of St. Joseph."[213] Humanly it could have seemed that the congregation of Oblates could not survive without him. Like St. Joseph, however, he never lost the awareness that he was an instrument, an "unprofitable servant,"[214] and God was the protagonist. Particularly during the last year of his life, the above-mentioned crisis with the Little House became so acute that he observed an increasing "spiritual darkness" leaving the brothers on very unsure ground. His response, however, was: "Bless-

---

[212] *"Dabit D.nus intercedente B. Josepho."* Letter 251, 3/22/1893.

[213] *"... un solo fine: il servizio di Dio nell'imitazione di S. Giuseppe."* Letter 207, 3/7/1891.

[214] *"Servus inutilis,"* Luke !7:10.

ed be also the frightful darkness, if it is the will of the Lord that sends it. We shall walk trustingly in the dark."[215]

Because of his prodigious activity and his serene uncomplaining speech, few people were aware of the poor health that Marello endured from the days of his youth when he almost died of typhoid. In May of 1895, in the midst of this crisis for his congregation, he accepted the invitation to travel to Savona to speak for the third centenary of St. Philip Neri's death. Taken ill while there, he nevertheless went in pilgrimage to the nearby Shrine of Our Lady of Mercy, spending the entire morning in prayer there. It is believed that here he offered his life "for the survival and growth of his dear congregation."[216] This attitude of self-sacrifice is final confirmation of his total confidence that the congregation was God's work and not his own. Marello faded from the scene in the same manner that St. Joseph vanished from Christ's life. His congregation came through the crisis and grew according to the dictates of providence. Marello's sacrifice proved acceptable in the eyes of the Lord.

---

[215] "E siano benedette anche queste paurose tenebre se le addensa la volontà del Signore. Cammineremo fiduciosamente nel buio...." Letter 272, 11/26/1894.

[216] "... il sacrificio della sua vita per il trionfo e la prosperità della sua cara Congregazione." CORTONA, Brief Memories, ch. 12.

Why is Marello "Blessed"? Because he not only had a great affection for and a great devotion to St. Joseph, but most of all because he imitated his virtues.[217] Marello is Blessed because he learned and attained holiness at the school of St. Joseph, a sure model of holiness for all.

---

[217] "*La devozione del Servo di Dio a S. Giuseppe era una devozione di grande affetto, ma soprattutto di imitazione.*" Garberoglio in *Positio Super Intro.*, 175.

APPENDIX I

VATICAN DECREES ON THE HOLINESS OF BLESSED SERRA AND BLESSED MARELLO

DECREE ON THE HEROIC VIRTUES OF THE SERVANT OF GOD, JUNIPERO SERRA, GRANTING HIM THE TITLE "VENERABLE"

Mindful[218] of the words of Jesus Christ, St. Francis of Assisi sent his brothers into the world, saying: "Go, dearly beloved, two by two into different parts of the world, announcing to people peace and repentance for the remission of sins; and be patient in tribulation, with the assurance that the Lord will fulfill his purpose and promise. Reply humbly to those who question you, bless those who persecute you, give thanks to those who inflict injury and calumny against you, for, in view of this, an eternal kingdom is prepared for us." (Thomas of Celano, *Vita Prima Sancti Francisci Assisiensis*, XII, 29).

These exhortations were carried out in his missionary work by the Servant of God Junipero

---

[218]Translation of this decree and of the following one from Latin is by Rev. Paul J. Pavese, O.S.J.

Serra, an illustrious member of the Friars Minor, a fearless herald of the Gospel, who with zealous concern and at the cost of many hardships established the Church in the vast regions of North America. Driven by an intense zeal for the salvation of souls and for the spread of God's kingdom, he gave clear witness that the Church, the mother and teacher of all nations, reached out through her children to men of every condition, especially the poor and the afflicted, and that he willingly spent himself for them to promote their human dignity, spiritual renewal, and social progress (cf. Vat. II, Decree on the Missionary Activity of the Church, *Ad Gentes*, 12).

The Servant of God, Junipero Serra, was born in Petra, the major Balearic Island, on November 24, 1713, to a simple but truly Christian family, where he received a sound religious education.

In 1730 he asked to enter the Order of Friars Minor, and on September 14 of that same year he entered the novitiate in the monastery of Our Lady of the Angels in Palma, Mallorca. There he was attracted to the study of the annals of the Order, especially the missionary apostolate to which so many of his associates had dedicated themselves in the course of the centuries. From that time on he was consumed by the desire to emulate their deeds as a missionary among non-Christians.

On September 15, 1731, he made his religious profession, replacing the name of Miguel José that had been given to him in baptism with that of Junipero. This name had been made famous by that Franciscan who the Seraphic Founder himself affirmed had reached the perfect state of patience by renouncing his will and by his ardent desire to imitate Christ by following the way of the cross (cf. *Speculum Perfectionis*, 85).

He studied philosophy (1731-34) and theology (1734-37) at the Franciscan monastery of Palma. He was ordained a deacon on March 17, 1736, and was later ordained to the priesthood.

On receiving faculties for preaching and for hearing confessions, he launched into the apostolate with great alacrity. For three years (1740-43) his superiors entrusted him with teaching philosophy in the monastery of St. Francis. There, after earning a doctoral degree in theology, he taught this subject at the University of Palma from 1744 to 1749.

Finally, after taking leave of his aging parents, whom he dearly loved, and bidding farewell to his confreres, whose feet he insisted on kissing, he departed for the missions on April 13, 1749. He arrived at Vera Cruz on December 7. He then proceeded on foot for Mexico City. On the way his left foot was infected by an ulcer, which became the cause of frequent inflammation of the bone and more or less affected his walking. The Servant of God bore this physical ailment bravely for the rest of his life, never complaining, and refusing any treatment even during his long journeys on foot.

In the month of June 1750, he volunteered for the missions of Sierra Gorda, where he remained eight years, tirelessly dedicated to the spread of the Gospel.

Forgetful of his physical sufferings and the hardship of travel, he visited many places to strengthen, support, and encourage his associates as well as the faithful. He built churches and from the year 1752 he exercised the office of Head of the Inquisition. His greatest and most successful work was in the area known as Jalpán. There he expended his best energies without interruption for the conversion of the Indians known as "Pames," and he built that mission into a model Christian community. He preached, catechized, baptized; he took care that his own life was a shining example to all, a life of outstanding faith, piety, penance, charity and poverty. He celebrated Mass with solemnity, he confessed his own sins in the sanctuary in the sight of the faithful so that they might frequent the

sacraments. He worked side by side with the build-
ers of that famous church which still stands today
as a supremely beautiful monument to his zeal. He
trained the Pames in temporal matters; he defended
their rights against the encroachments and abuses
of their masters. He dressed poorly and ate very
little.

Spurning all earthly desires and always ready to
obey, he left his mission by order of his superiors in
order to restore the mission of St. Saba in Texas,
which had been destroyed a short time before by
the Apaches. But he had to renounce this plan on
the advice of the Spanish authorities, who considered it to be extremely dangerous. So he was de-
tained in the religious community of San Fernando,
in Mexico City, where he alternated community life
in that residence with the preaching ministry in
many dioceses of Mexico. He excelled among all his
confreres for his customary religious fervor and for
his humility and the practice of penance.

He was always most observant of the Rules and
the Constitutions. He was frugal in food and sleep.
He spent much time in meditation and in devout
exercise of the Stations of the Cross.

Endowed in his preaching with the gifts of
eloquence, solid philosophical and theological

doctrine and knowledge of the Scripture, he spoke of heavenly things and he inveighed against vice.

In 1767, as head of several missionaries he set out to achieve his primary goal, that of bringing the Christian religion and life to California.

First he launched out in Lower California (1767-69). Next, in spite of his poor health and relying only on divine help, he was moved by his love for souls and for the glory of God to travel with other associates to Upper California. He bore hardships and faced many dangers and difficulties. In the end, he kindled the light of Christ and the fire of Christian charity in the hearts of tribes formerly primitive and pagan.

In the space of fifteen years he founded nine missions (San Diego, San Carlos Borromeo in the city of Monterey, San Antonio, San Gabriel, San Luis Obispo, San Francisco, San Juan Capistrano, Santa Clara, San Buenaventura) over a vast area through which he journeyed many times to preach the word of God, administer the sacraments, and defend the rights of the poor and lowly.

On account of the unjust encroachments of local authorities, he was obliged to undertake a harsh and laborious journey to Mexico City (1772-73) in order to explain the program of the missionaries and defend their rights. After successfully settling this matter, he returned to the city of Monterey, where he had to face other problems and persecutions too numerous to describe here. It is fitting, however, at least to mention that the Servant of God, while by nature excitable, showed, in every misfortune as well as in ordinary circumstances, great prudence, supreme obedience, perfect submission to God's will, and boundless trust in the help of grace.

In all things he sought only the good of his neighbor, for whose temporal and eternal salvation he suffered indignities, persecutions and sorrows, with the sole purpose of following the precepts of justice and charity according to his conscience.

His remarkable dedication to work, truly a sign of his lively faith, did not distract him from the interior life, nor from prayer, nor from union with God, nor from the observance of the Franciscan Rule.

He practiced patience up to the last days of his life. He yearned for martyrdom; he loved poverty, self-denial, the Church. He willingly forgave those who bothered him. With intense care he practiced humility. He strove with all his might for holiness and progressed rapidly in the way of evangelical perfection.

Broken in health and comforted by the sacrament of the anointing of the sick, he died a holy death in the city of Monterey on August 28, 1784, pressing to his heart the crucifix he wore as a missionary. The fame of sanctity which accompanied him in life remained after his death. And so in 1949 the Informative Process was introduced at the Monterey-Fresno Chancery. At the same time, the Process of Interrogation was set up in San Francisco and Los Angeles, California. The "Instruction on his Life and Virtues," handled by the historical-hagiographical Office of the Congregation for the Causes of the Saints, was published in 1981 and was approved by the Historical Consultors on February 17, 1982. Previously, on April 28, 1972, the decree of the Sacred Congregation had been issued on the writings attributed to the Servant of God.

After all preparations had been completed to discuss the virtues exercised by the Servant of God Junipero Serra, the Special Meeting of the Consultors was held on February 12, 1985, with the Promoter of the Faith presiding. Later on April 2 of that same year, the Ordinary Congregation of the Cardinals took place, His Eminence Joseph Cardinal Caprio presiding. In both meetings everyone declared that the Servant of God had practiced the theological and cardinal virtues and the virtues related to them, in a heroic degree.

All this having been presented to His Holiness John Paul II by the above mentioned Cardinal Prefect, the Sovereign Pontiff gladly acceded to the wishes of the Sacred Congregation and ordered that the decree on the virtues of the Servant be prepared. This having been duly completed, on this day, in the presence of the Cardinal Prefect, myself as Secretary, and with others present according to custom, the Holy Father solemnly declared: *It is certain that the theological virtues of Faith, Hope and Charity towards both God and neighbor, as well as the cardinal virtues of Prudence, Justice, Temperance and Fortitude and the related virtues, were exercised in a heroic degree by the Servant of God, Junipero Serra, a professed priest of the Order of Friars Minor, in the case and for the purpose in question.*

The Supreme Pontiff ordered this decree to be recorded in the acts of the Sacred Congregation and to be made public.

Given in Rome, May 9, 1985.

Signed:
Pietro Cardinal Palazzini, Prefect
†Troianus Crisan, Archbishop

THE HONORS OF THE BLESSED BESTOWED ON JUNIPERO SERRA

JOHN PAUL II
in lasting memory

"Jesus now called the Twelve together and gave them power and authority to overcome all the demons and to cure diseases. He sent them forth to proclaim the reign of God and heal the afflicted. Jesus advised them: "Take nothing for the journey, neither walking staff nor traveling bag; no bread, no money. No one is to have two coats.... So they set out and went from village to village, spreading the good news everywhere and curing diseases." (Lk 9:1-3,6).

These words, with which the Lord Jesus entrusted to the Twelve the task of announcing the Good News and of healing the diseases of the brethren they might meet on the way, were clearly understood and put into action by the Servant of God, Friar Junipero Miguel José Serra Ferrer, a priest of the Order of Friars Minor. There is no doubt that he pondered these words at length and recognized in them the spirit with which Francis of

Assisi, the founder of the Order to which he belonged, willed to send his friars everywhere.

He was born at Petra, on the island of Mallorca, on November 24, 1713, to a family of farmers and was given the name Miguel José on the day of his baptism. On entering the Order of Friars Minor in 1730, he took the name of Junipero. After his ordination to the priesthood in 1737, he taught philosophy and theology. At the same time he did not neglect the pastoral ministry, especially that of preaching, in which he soon achieved outstanding fame.

In 1749 he volunteered to go to Mexico and, soon after his arrival, was assigned to the mission that would be known as Sierra Gorda, located northeast of Mexico City. The Servant of God served as novice master for nine years, while at the same time exercising his beloved preaching apostolate. In 1767 he was appointed superior of the missions of Lower California, and scarcely two years later he crossed over to Upper California (what is now called the state of California). There, chiefly under his leadership, were established the missions of San Diego, San Carlos Borromeo, San Antonio, San Gabriel, San Luis Obispo, San Francisco, San Juan Capistrano, Santa Clara, and San Buenaventura.

Disagreements that arose between the missionaries and the viceroy of Spain in California prompted Fray Junipero to draw up a "Constitution of the Rights of Indians," which secured for him the office of both governing and educating the Indians who had been baptized.

In all the missions Fray Junipero and his brethren trained the Indians to cultivate the land and to use natural resources to raise their standard of living.

His love for the Indians was one of intense dedication. It was evangelical love which flowed from a life of total self-denial and from a spirit of reconciliation and peace that embraced both Christian and pagan Indians. The words he wrote to the viceroy can be considered the foundation of his life and his spiritual testament: "If perchance either Christian or pagan Indians kill me, they must be forgiven.... The killer must be led to understand that he is forgiven so that the Christian law may be fulfilled which desires not the death of the sinner but his salvation."

Fray Junipero spent the last years of his life in governing the missions and in writing letters to all missionaries in his desire to establish new missions. He died on August 28, 1778, in the San Carlos mission. He was mourned by all, especially the

Indians, as their "Blessed Father." He spent thirty-four years in the work of the missions, drawing his strength from lifting his mind to him who was nailed to the cross and who suffered unspeakable torments for the salvation of mankind. Indeed, his great charity made a deep impression on both young and old, who came to know him and regard him as a saint and genuine apostle.

The fame of his sanctity has remained constantly alive and has increased steadily to this day. From 1948 to 1949 the informative process was held in the diocese of Monterey and Los Angeles, California.

In 1981 the historical and hagiographical study of his life and virtues was published by the Sacred Congregation for the Causes of Saints. Then, as required by law, that same Congregation examined the virtues of the Servant of God. On March 9, 1985, we ourselves declared these virtues to be heroic.

The miracle for the beatification of the Servant of God took place in St. Paul's Hospital, located in St. Louis, in the United States. The beneficiary of this miracle was a nun named Sister Boniface Dyrda.

In accordance with the rules, we declared the genuineness of the miracle on December 11, 1987.

Finally, we set the date of the beatification for September 25, 1988, in St. Peter's Square, in Rome.

Therefore, today during the liturgy we made the following statement:

"In fulfillment of the wishes of our brothers Sergio Obeso Rivers, Archbishop of Jalapa; Luigi Bommarito, Archbishop of Catania; Anastasio Alberto Ballestrero, Archbishop of Turin; Thaddeus Shubsda, Bishop of Monterey, California; Lawrence Noel, Bishop of Three Rivers, Canada; Miguel Roca Cabanellas, Archbishop of Valencia, and of many other brother bishops, and of many of the faithful; after consulting the Sacred Congregation for the Causes of Saints; by virtue of our apostolic authority we grant that the Venerable Servants of God: Miguel Agustín Pro, Joseph Benedict Dusmet, Francesco Faà di Bruno, Junípero Miguel José Serra Ferrer, Frederick Janssoone Bollengier, Josephine Naval Girbés, shall be called "Blessed" in the future, and that their feast shall be celebrated on the day of their birth: Miguel Agustín Pro, on November 23; Joseph Benedict Dusmet, on April 4; Francesco Faà di Bruno on March 27; Junípero Miguel José Serra Ferrer, on August 28; Frederick Janssoone Bollengier, on August 4; Josephine Naval Girbés, on February 24, in the places and in the

manner established by law. In the name of the Father and of the Son and of the Holy Spirit."

After this pronouncement we were the first to invoke the new blesseds and to propose their virtues for imitation by the faithful. At the same time we implored God to raise up continually in his Church, the faithful mother of saints, other men and women like them, who by their shining example shall show the way of salvation to their brethren as they strive with sincere hearts and through many trials to reach the heavenly kingdom.

What we have decreed, we wish to remain in force now and in the future, not withstanding anything to the contrary.

Given in Rome, at St. Peter's, under the seal of the Fisherman, on September 25 of the year 1988, the tenth of our pontificate.

†Agostino Cardinal Casaroli
Secretary of State

DECREE ON THE HEROIC VIRTUES OF THE SERVANT OF GOD JOSEPH MARELLO GRANTING HIM THE TITLE "VENERABLE"

"St. Joseph is the model of the humble, whom Christianity raises to great destinies; St. Joseph is the proof that to be good and authentic followers of Christ, great things are not necessary, but what are sufficient and necessary are the common virtues, human and simple, but true and authentic" (Paul VI, Allocution of March 19, 1969).

To have perceived this truth, to have made it a principle of life for himself and for others, to have personally experienced it was the charism and commitment of Joseph Marello, founder of the Oblates of St. Joseph and Bishop of Acqui.

Joseph Marello was born in Turin on December 26, 1844, the son of Vincenzo Marello and Anna Maria Viale. After the premature death of his mother, he was moved at a tender age to be with his grandparents in San Martino Alfieri. On October 31, 1856, he passed from there to the Asti Seminary. His vocation encountered trials, but also dedication, evidenced by notable advancement in his studies, spirituality, discipline and moral conduct.

Priest

When he became a priest on September 19, 1868, his bishop, Carlo Savio, chose him to be his secretary and was able to experience his interiority, his application to ecclesiastical studies, his prudence in administration, his zealous trustworthiness in keeping secrets, his docility and kind manner. Given his extraordinary inclination to virtue, Marello greatly profited from Bishop Savio's profound school of priestly life. He so progressed in the spirit of meekness and humility as to become admired by whoever drew near him.

The First Vatican Council, which he attended with his Bishop, enriched his ecclesial experience, which during the pontificate of Pius IX came to be expressed in the three great proclamations of the Immaculate Conception, the infallibility of the Pope, and the Patronage of St. Joseph.

Bishop Savio's esteem for Marello grew to the point of choosing him as his confessor and as his heir. Through the various responsibilities entrusted to him in the diocese, others too could admire what a "precious gem of a priest" he was. From 1881 until the time of his appointment as bishop, he exercised the office of chancellor of the curia with exceptional prudence and skill.

From 1880 until 1882 he was spiritual director of the seminary, where by his teachings and above all by his example he had a powerful influence in awaking a spirit of devotion among the seminarians. In 1880 he also was appointed effective canon of the cathedral church, assuming in 1886 the second highest chapter position, that of archdeacon. Appointed pro-synodal examiner in 1887, he exhibited vast moral learning in the correct appraisal of the candidates.

In 1883, together with other canons, he acquired the large building of Santa Chiara to move a charitable hospice there. Two years later he freely offered to go live there in the midst of that family of marginalized people, which had grown to over two hundred, so as to better attend to their spiritual and material needs. He thus dedicated himself and his income to a work lacking in financial security.

Gifted with outstanding efficiency, he was able to unite peacefulness and constancy. He fulfilled all his duties with both a dignified calm and firmness, earning the esteem and respect of all, while never straying from the path of duty.

Reserved, humble and modest, he was always most careful about judging or speaking about his neighbor. Notwithstanding his frequent contacts with the clergy and with all types of people, no one ever saw him look irritated or speak harshly. He was always patient and meek of soul.

He expressed his deep faith in his prayer and in the most edifying demeanor at all the sacred ceremonies. His zeal was manifest in the promotion of many pious devotions, especially in the church adjoining the hospice. Through his initiative, the practice of the devotion to Most Holy Mary, the Queen of hearts, according to the method of St. Louis Mary Grignon de Montfort, was introduced into Asti after Rome.

Conscious of collaborating with the Savior in the work of conversion, he attended to the Sacrament of Penance daily, morning and evening, in the cathedral church, in the seminary, and in other institutes. He preached spontaneously and frequently, and people enjoyed listening to his eloquence filled with deep and gentle learning. In this way his love for God was translated daily into service to his brethren, hiding the extraordinary practice of virtue under the purest modesty.

Founder

Inspired by the example of St. Joseph, who in silent humility had cooperated in the mystery of the

Incarnation, Marello took him as the model of his interior life and also of his priestly ministry, which like that of St. Joseph "is a ministry of intimate relationship with the divine Word."

Moved by the Holy Spirit to transmit this ideal of life to others, he founded the Oblates of St. Joseph on March 14, 1878, so that they might imitate the virtues of this saint, spread his devotion, and lend their humble service to the local church as catechists and ministers of divine worship.

Even when providence later disposed that his institute be transformed from lay into clerical, he kept the same program of availability to the service of the diocese. He wanted the Oblates to recognize the church as the very body of Christ and to continue to serve his interests. This was to be done in the humble and hard-working spirit with which St. Joseph attended to Christ's physical body and became a loving servant of whatever would be required by the presence of the Messiah in his home.

In Marello's understanding, the style of Josephite apostolate will always remain flexible, humble and selfless, content with whatever the Lord assigns.

The congregation of the Oblates of St. Joseph was approved by the Bishop of Asti on March 18, 1901 and by the Holy See on April 11, 1909. In this same spirit it has now spread throughout Italy, in the Americas, and in the Far East.

Bishop

At 43 years of age and 19 as a priest, Marello was appointed Bishop of Acqui. His episcopal ordination took place at Rome on February 17, 1889.

Fully appreciative of the office of bishop, he manifested the presence of Christ to all, who came to recognize and love him as leader and father, because he had become a visible servant (cf. Luke 22:26f; *Lumen Gentium* III, 21,27).

"He became an example to the flock" (1 Peter 5:3), leading clergy and faithful to the highest sanctity. With renewed zeal and apostolic spirit he consecrated himself totally to the spiritual welfare of his diocese, dedicating particular care to the seminary, to clergy and to religious. He promoted the sacraments, sacred preaching, and catechesis.

He visited every corner of his diocese, at the cost of great sacrifice due to his poor health and to the distance and discomfort of travel. He edified all with his prayer, preaching, attention to the poor, the sick and children, who instinctively recognized in his kindness the image of Jesus the good shepherd (cf. John 10:1-16; 1 Peter 2:25).

He always faithfully imitated St. Joseph, the model of his interior life, in the constant and heroic exercise of the hidden and common virtues. The fruit of this was seen in his equanimity and total conformity to the will of God, even amidst serious difficulties which he had to confront both for the unity of his diocese and for the survival of the congregation of the Oblates. Although he only remained six years in the diocese, the splendor of his virtues and the prudence of his administration caused Leo XIII to call him "a pearl of a bishop." In his diocese he is remembered as "most meek of soul and endowed with the extraordinary virtue of calming others, most admired by all for the gentleness of his countenance and his speech."

Although he was sick, he went to Savona on a pastoral mission. On May 30, 1895, he unexpectedly died there, a victim of his charity. He had celebrated his last Mass at the Shrine of Our Lady of Mercy, to whom he had entrusted his episcopal ministry, writing on his coat of arms: "Prepare a safe journey."

Priests and bishops above all find in Joseph Marello a great model of spirituality, which will allow them in this externally oriented society to maintain that balance required by the economy of the redemption and to integrate the interior life with the exterior, uniting divine action with human efforts.

The Cause for Beatification

The fame of sanctity was already asserted during the lifetime of the Servant of God. After his death it spread and appeared to be confirmed by God by heavenly signs. The Cause was therefore initiated to grant him the honors of the Blessed.

Hence, during 1924-1928 and 1941-1942 in the diocesan curia of Acqui the informative proceedings were held to examine the fame of sanctity of the Servant of God, his writings, and the absence of unapproved liturgical devotion to him. Similar proceedings were held in the curia of Asti during 1924-1928, and by written request in the archdiocesan curia of Turin in 1925.

The documents of the proceedings were forwarded to Rome, and on May 28, 1948 in accord with the canonical norms, Pius XII personally signed the decree for the introduction of the Cause.

Subsequently, during 1948-1951 by apostolic authority, there was held in the curia of Acqui the process on the individual virtues of the Servant of God. The juridical validity of the above proceedings was attested to by the Decree of the Sacred Congregation of Rites, dated March 17, 1954.

Afterwards, the Sacred Congregation for the Causes of the Saints held discussions on the theological and cardinal virtues, as well as related virtues of the Servant of God, Joseph Marello. On October 25, 1977 the Official Prelates and Consulting Fathers met first in Special Congress. Then the Plenary Congregation met under the chairmanship of His Eminence Cardinal Luigi Ciappi, and their Eminences the Cardinals gave their votes. Having thoroughly examined everything, it was unanimously agreed that the Servant of God had exercised all the Christian virtues to a heroic degree.

Once the undersigned Cardinal Prefect had presented a faithful report of all this to the Supreme Pontiff Paul VI, during the audience of April 13 of this current year 1978, His Holiness confirmed the votes of their Eminences, the Cardinal Fathers, and ordered that there be prepared the decree on the heroic virtues of the Servant of God.

Heroic Practice of Virtue

When this was properly done, on this day there gathered myself, Cardinal Luigi Ciappi, the proponent and chairman of the Cause; the undersigned Secretary of this Sacred Congregation, and other officials. In our presence the Supreme Pontiff himself declared: *It is established that the Servant of God, Joseph Marello, Bishop of Acqui, founder of the Congregation of the Oblates of St. Joseph, of Asti, exercised the theological virtues of Faith, Hope and Charity, both towards God and neighbor, and also the cardinal virtues of Prudence, Justice, Temperance and Fortitude, and other related virtues to a heroic degree.*

The Pontiff himself ordered this Decree to be promulgated and inserted among the Acts of the Sacred Congregation for the Causes of the Saints.

Rome, June 12, 1978 A.D.

Signed and sealed
        Conrad Card. Bafile, Prefect
        † Joseph Casoria, Archbp.

BEATIFICATION DECREE OF THE VENERABLE SERVANT OF GOD JOSEPH MARELLO BISHOP AND FOUNDER

JOHN PAUL II
for perpetual memory

"Whoever remains in me, and I in him, bears much fruit" (John 15:5).

This evangelical promise has again been realized in a marvelous way, in the life and apostolate of Bishop Joseph Marello. He cultivated intimate union with God and, having in himself the same sentiments as Christ Jesus (Philippians 2:5), he worked with constant commitment and ardent zeal for the advent of the kingdom of God in the world. He obtained abundant spiritual fruits.

This great shepherd of souls was born in Turin on December 26, 1844.

Orphaned of his mother during childhood, he entrusted himself to the protection of his heavenly Mother, who became the guide of his vocation. In the diocesan seminary of Asti he undertook the road toward the priesthood, not without experiencing difficult moments, which helped mature him interiorly and strengthen his commitment to the service of God and neighbor with holiness and competence.

His superiors and companions thus grew to esteem him ever more. He formed deep bonds of friendship with some of them in particular, which led them to adopt a rule of life and to live it together.

He was ordained a priest on September 19, 1868, and the Bishop of Asti, Carlo Savio, chose him as his secretary and later as his confessor.

He thus had the opportunity for new and profound experiences. From Savio he learned the inexhaustible capacity for self-giving, transforming his arid task of secretary into an apprenticeship for apostolic service.

He broadened his apostolate, dedicating himself to teaching catechism, to spiritual direction, to the apostolate of good publications, to the education of youth.

Accompanying his Bishop on his pastoral visits, he saw the urgency of helping the clergy in the parish apostolate.

He made his own the concern of the bishops of his time to introduce the evangelical leaven into society with the help of laity joined together in Catholic associations.

At the same time he cultivated in his heart the earnest desire to consecrate himself to the Lord in a Trappist monastery.

Although he was not to realize this desire of his because God called him to another vocation, he nevertheless communicated his yearning for consecration to the Lord to other youth by founding the congregation of the Oblates of St. Joseph. In this way, in the city of Asti he brought about a rebirth of the experience of male religious life, which had been abolished by the suppressive laws of the time.

He invited his Oblates to express in their own lives and apostolate the Christian mystery as lived by St. Joseph in union with God, in humility, in hiddenness, in hard work.

He used to say: "We should draw inspiration from St. Joseph, who was the first on earth to look after the interests of Jesus. He guarded him in his infancy, protected him in his boyhood and acted as his father during the first thirty years of his life on earth."

He wanted his spiritual sons above all to care for the moral and religious education of youth, especially through catechesis, and pastoral ministry in parishes.

His light soon had to shine from a candlestick. In fact the Supreme Pontiff Leo XIII appointed him

Bishop of Acqui. The priests and faithful of this diocese admired his immeasurable faith, his unlimited pastoral charity, his kindness to all, his humility, patience and spirit of prayer, to the point that he was revered as a new St. Francis de Sales.

He felt like an "Oblate" and he lived as an "Oblate": that is, completely consecrated to God and committed to his people. His actions, words and writings witnessed to the kindness of the Heavenly Father to all, and to youth in particular.

With dedication and a spirit of sacrifice he visited all the parishes of his diocese, heedless of discomforts.

To him, as to the good shepherd, the faithful flocked for counsel and assistance. They trustingly brought their sick children for him to bless.

Because of his apostolic zeal and his outstanding virtues, Pope Leo XIII called him "a Pearl of a Bishop" and Pius X "the Saintly Bishop."

After only six years in the episcopate, on May 30, 1895, death seized him at Savona. Notwithstanding his precarious health condition, he had gone there for the celebration of the third centenary of the death of St. Philip Neri.

His fame of sanctity endured after his death, and was confirmed by numerous favors attributed to his intercession. His Cause for Canonization was initiated with the opening of the ordinary informative proceedings.

Once the juridical proceedings were successfully completed, on June 12, 1978 the Supreme Pontiff Paul VI declared that Bishop Joseph Marello had cultivated to a heroic degree the theological and cardinal virtues and those related to them.

In 1991 there took place in Asti the canonical process regarding an allegedly miraculous healing that had occurred in 1944 and was attributed to the intercession of the Venerable Servant of God. Subjected to careful examination, the case obtained a favorable judgement, and on April 2, 1993, a decree on the miracle was issued.

Consequently, we have determined that the rite of Beatification be celebrated in Asti, during our pastoral visit to that beloved diocese.

Today, therefore, in this city just mentioned, during the solemn celebration of Mass, we have pronounced this formula:

"Embracing the desire of our brother Severino Poletto, Bishop of Asti and of many other brothers in the Episcopate, of the entire religious family of the Oblates of St. Joseph, and of many of the faithful and after having received the favorable response of the Congregation for the Cause of the Saints, we grant with our apostolic authority that the Venera-

ble Servant of God, Joseph Marello, Bishop of Acqui and Founder of the Oblates of St. Joseph, henceforth be called Blessed, and that his Feast Day be celebrated, in the places and according to the norms established by Church Law, every year on May 30, the date of his birth into Heaven. In the name of the Father and of the Son and of the Holy Spirit."

What we have decreed in this Letter we wish to be ratified and confirmed now and in the future, notwithstanding any decision to the contrary.

From Asti, with the seal of the Fisherman, September 26, 1993, the fifteenth year of our pontificate.

Signed and Sealed
        Angelo Card. Sodano, Secretary of State

138

APPENDIX II

PRAYERS
TO
SAINT JOSEPH,
BLESSED SERRA
AND
BLESSED MARELLO

SAINT JOSEPH PRAYERS

The Seven Sorrows and Joys of St. Joseph

I *Chaste Lover of Mary, how overwhelmed you were when you thought that you would have to end your betrothal to her. But when the angel of God came to you in a dream, you were filled with awe to realize that Mary would be your wife, and you would be the guardian of the Messiah.*

Help us St. Joseph, help our families and all our loved ones to overcome all sadness of heart and develop an absolute trust in God's goodness.

II *Faithful guardian of Jesus, what a failure you thought you were when you could only provide a stable for the birth of the Holy Child. And then what a wonder it was when shepherds came to tell of angel choirs, and wise men came to adore the King of Kings.*

Through your example and prayers, help us St. Joseph and all we love to become like sinless mangers where the Savior of the world may be received with absolute love and respect.

III *Tender-hearted Joseph, you too felt pain when the blood of Jesus was first shed at His circumcision. Yet how proud you were to be the one privileged to give the name Jesus, Savior, to the very Son of God.*

Pray for us St. Joseph, that the sacred blood of Christ, poured out for our salvation, may guard our families, so the Divine Name of Jesus may be written in our hearts forever.

IV *Joseph, loving husband, how bewildered you were when Simeon spoke the words of warning that the hearts of Jesus and Mary would be pierced with sorrows. Yet his prediction that this would lead to the salvation of innumerable souls filled you with consolation.*

Help us, St. Joseph, to see with eyes of faith that even the sorrows and pains of those we deeply love can become the pathway to salvation and eternal life.

V *Courageous protector of the Holy Family, how terrified you were when you had to make the sudden flight with Jesus and Mary to escape the treachery of King Herod and the cruelty of his soldiers. But when you reached Egypt, what satisfaction you had to know that the Savior of the world had come to replace the pagan idols.*

Teach us by your example, St. Joseph, to keep far from the false idols of earthly attractions, so that like you, we may be entirely devoted to the service of Jesus and Mary.

VI *Ever-obedient Joseph, you trustingly returned to Nazareth at God's command, in spite of your fear that King Herod's son might still be a threat to Jesus' life. Then what fatherly pride you had in seeing Jesus grow in wisdom and grace before God and men under your care.*

Show us St. Joseph, how to be free from all useless fear and worry, so we may enjoy the peace of a tranquil conscience, living safely with Jesus and Mary in our hearts.

VII *Dependable father and husband, how frantic you and Mary were when, through no fault of yours, you searched for three days to find Jesus. What incredible relief was yours when you found Him safe in the Temple of God.*

Help us St. Joseph, never to lose Jesus through the fault of our own sins. But if we should lose Him, lead us back with unwearied sorrow, until we find Him again; so that we, like you, may finally pass from this life, dying safely in the arms of Jesus and Mary.

Invocation to St. Joseph by Blessed Joseph Marello

Oh Glorious Saint Joseph, after the Blessed Virgin, you were the first to hold in your arms the Redeemer. Be our exemplar in our ministry, which like your own, is a ministry of intimate relationship with

the Divine Word. May you teach us; may you
assist us; may you make us worthy members of the
Holy Family.

Prayer of Pope Leo XIII to St. Joseph after the Marian Rosary[219]

To you, Oh Blessed Joseph, we come in our trials, and
having asked the help of your most holy spouse, we
confidently ask your patronage also. Through that
sacred bond of charity which united you to the
Immaculate Virgin Mother of God and through the
fatherly love with which you embraced the Child
Jesus, we humbly beg you to look graciously upon
the beloved inheritance which Jesus Christ pur-
chased by his blood, and to aid us in our necessities
with your power and strength.

Oh most provident guardian of the Holy Family,
defend the chosen children of Jesus Christ. Most
beloved father, dispel the evil of falsehood and sin.
Our most mighty protector, graciously assist us
from heaven in our struggle with the powers of
darkness. And just as you once saved the Child
Jesus from mortal danger, so now defend God's
Holy Church from the snares of her enemies and
from all adversity. Shield each one of us by your

---

[219]Cf. John Paul II, *Redemptoris Custos*, Sec. 31.

constant protection, so that, supported by your example and your help, we may be able to live a virtuous life, to die a holy death, and to obtain eternal happiness in heaven. Amen.

St. Joseph Rosary

May be prayed just as Marian rosary, substituting "Hail Mary" with the following:

Joseph, son of David, and husband of Mary; we honor you, guardian of the Redeemer, and we adore the child you named Jesus.

Saint Joseph, patron of the universal church, pray with us, that we may imitate you in lifelong dedication to the interests of the Savior. Amen.

Mysteries
1) Betrothal to Mary *(Mt 1:18)*.
2) Annunciation to Joseph *(Mt 1:19-21)*.
3) Birth and Naming of Jesus *(Mt 1:22-25)*.
4) Flight into Egypt *(Mt 2:13-15)*.
5) Hidden Life at Nazareth *(Mt 2:23; Lk 2:51-52)*.

BLESSED SERRA PRAYERS

Oration from Blessed Serra Liturgy

God, most high, your servant Junipero Serra brought the gospel of Christ to the peoples of Mexico and California and firmly established the Church among them. By his intercession, and through the example of his evangelical zeal, inspire us to be faithful witnesses of Jesus Christ, who lives and reigns with you and the Holy Spirit, one God, for ever and ever.

Prayer in honor of Blessed Serra

Oh God, in your ineffable mercy, you chose Blessed Junipero Serra as a means of gathering many peoples of the Americas into your Church. Grant that through his intercession our hearts may be united to you in ever greater love so that at all times and in all places we may show forth the image of your Only-Begotten Son, our Lord Jesus Christ, who lives and reigns with you in the unity of the Holy Spirit, one God, for ever and ever.

Prayer to Blessed Serra

Blessed Junipero, you served God with humble confidence on earth and because "whoever humbles himself will be exalted," you now enjoy his beatific vision. We thank God for raising you to the rank of Blessed so that more people will draw near and imitate you, seek your powerful help, and in so doing will humble themselves and so be exalted with you in eternal glory, through Christ our Lord.

BLESSED MARELLO PRAYERS

Oration from Blessed Marello Liturgy

Oh God, You inspired in Blessed Bishop Joseph Marello the ardent desire to express by his interior life and in his apostolate the Christian mystery as lived by St. Joseph, guardian of the Redeemer: by his intercession grant that we may imitate him in his intimate union with you and in his zeal for the service of the Church. We ask this through Christ, our Lord. Amen.

Prayer to Blessed Marello[220]

Oh Blessed Joseph Marello, like your patron and model St. Joseph, you are proof that sanctity consists not in extraordinary achievements that attract the world's attention, but in the daily exercise of the virtues of simplicity, charity and humility. With complete trust in Divine Providence, you founded the Oblates of St. Joseph to serve the interests of Jesus in imitation of His guardian and protector. Father of youth, protector of the poor and aged, gentle shepherd of your flock, model of charity, you blended strength with kindness, prayer with action, and faithfulness to the Church with zealous attention to the signs of the times.

May your holy life inspire youth to take the Gospel as their sure guide; your Oblates to be hidden and faithful instruments of God's work; Priests and Bishops to be loyal and loving shepherds. Pray with us that we may all live with that peacefulness of mind and heart that comes only from a trusting surrender to God's will. Amen.

---

[220] Approved by Most Rev. Severino Poletto, Bishop of Asti, Italy, March 14, 1994.

OTHER GUARDIAN OF THE REDEEMER PUBLICATIONS

Joseph in the New Testament, 156 pp. by Fr. Larry Toschi, O.S.J. $10.95

Brief Memories of the Life of Joseph Marello, 172 pp. By Fr. Cortona, O.S.J. $8.95

"I, the undersigned poor sinner, ...", 249 pp. life of Bl. Marello by Giovanni Sisto $9.95

Blessed Joseph Marello, A Life for God and Neighbor, 32 pp. by Verna & Citera $2.95

Holiness in the Ordinary, 117 pp. essays on Marellian spirituality by three O.S.J. $7.95

The Life of Blessed Joseph Marello in Pictures, 108 pp. color $14.95

Los Escritos y Las Enseñanzas del Bienaventurado J. Marello, 292 págs. $14.95

Bits of Gold, 45 pp. maxims of Bl. Marello for each day of the year $2.50

Pastoral Letter on the Catechism, 12 pp. by Blessed Joseph Marello $1.50

*Family of St. Joseph Prayer Manual, 48 pp. by the Oblates $3.00

O.S.J. History of the Congregation 1878-1993, 242 pp. by Fr. Siro Dal Degan, O.S.J. $29.95

Nathanael and the Child, 41 pp. 3 illustrated Christmas stories by Fr. Dal Degan, O.S.J. $8.00

A Letter on the Love of the Catholic Church, 69 pp. by Fr. Dal Degan, O.S.J. $5.95

Clarifications on Some Matters of Catholic Teaching, 61 pp.,
    by Fr. Dal Degan, O.S.J. $6.50
+Holy Spouses, color card with Holy Spouses Rosary
    . . . . 35¢ (50 for $10)
Father's Day, color card with prayer
    . . . . 35¢ (50 for $10)
Holy Family, color card with prayer
    . . . . 35¢ (50 for $10)
St. Joseph Protector of Church, card w/ St. Joseph Rosary
    30¢ (50 for $5)
St. Joseph the Worker, color card with prayer
    . . . . 30¢ (50 for $8)
+Blessed Joseph Marello, color card with prayer to him
    . . . . 35¢ (50 for $10)
San José en la Historia de la Salvación, 110 págs por P.
Stramare, O.S.J. $6.00

Items marked with * are also available in Spanish, and those marked with + are also available in Italian.
    Order from:

Guardian of the Redeemer Books,
544 West Cliff Drive,
Santa Cruz, CA   95060-6147
(408) 457-1868.

Include shipping and handling fees of $3 for first book and $1 for each additional book, counting 100 cards as one book. California residents add 8.25% sales tax.